OUTDATED

why
DATING
is Ruining your
LOVE
LIFE

SAMHITA
MUKHOPADHYAY

SEAL PRESS

OUTDATED

Why Dating Is Ruining Your Love Life

Published by
Seal Press
A Member of the Perseus Books Group
1700 Fourth Street
Berkeley, California

Library of Congress Cataloging-in-Publication Data

Mukhopadhyay, Samhita.
  Outdated : why dating is ruining your love life / Samhita Mukhopadhyay.
     p. cm.
  Includes bibliographical references.
  ISBN 978-1-58005-332-7
  1. Single women. 2. Dating (Social customs) 3. Feminism. I. Title.
  HQ800.2.M85 2011
  306.73—dc22

                              2011016197

9 8 7 6 5 4 3 2 1

Cover and interior design by Domini Dragoone
Printed in the United States of America
Distributed by Publishers Group West

To Ma,

for sacrificing everything so I could have the opportunity to ask the questions you never had the luxury to ask. (I also dedicate this to you with the hope that you don't kill me after reading its contents.)

CONTENTS

My motto, as I live and learn, is:
Dig and Be Dug In Return.
—Langston Hughes

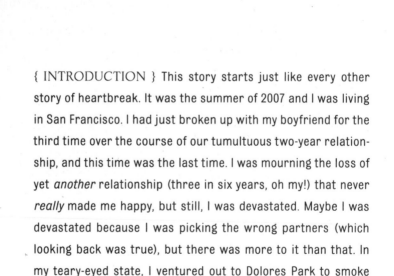

THE (NEW) PROBLEM
That Has NO NAME

{ INTRODUCTION } This story starts just like every other story of heartbreak. It was the summer of 2007 and I was living in San Francisco. I had just broken up with my boyfriend for the third time over the course of our tumultuous two-year relationship, and this time was the last time. I was mourning the loss of yet *another* relationship (three in six years, oh my!) that never *really* made me happy, but still, I was devastated. Maybe I was devastated because I was picking the wrong partners (which looking back was true), but there was more to it than that. In my teary-eyed state, I ventured out to Dolores Park to smoke cigarettes, pondering my last few years of constant heartbreak and feeling especially sorry for myself. (Like I said, this story starts like every other story.) I looked around me at a handful of happy couples and thought what every newly heartbroken person thinks: *What (the fuck) is wrong with me?*

I hurried to the bookstore, like I always do when I'm sad and looking for some escape or commiseration. I've always been drawn to bookstores during times of heartbreak. Usually, I am comforted or distracted enough by others' testimonials to love gone bad that I forget the stinging pain of a new breakup for a few hours.

But this time something was different. This time a trip to the bookstore didn't make me feel better because I was upset with more than just the end of the relationship. I needed something more this time. I was looking for a paradigm shift.

As I browsed through the enormous section on dating and self-help (all eight shelves, I kid you not), I saw book after book telling women what they were doing wrong, what they failed to understand, or what they needed to do better to make their relationships work. Almost all the books on the shelf were geared toward women (men's dating books do exist, but more on that later). What I was seeing in front of me, however, was an industry unchecked, overflowing with pages and pages of advice claiming to hold the secrets to your love life, implicitly—and often explicitly—linking a woman's very identity with her romantic status, equating her romantic success with her success as a woman.

As I skimmed through book after book (it was a long day), I realized these books, which claimed to be new and revolutionary, trailblazing, and mind-blowing, were merely echoing mainstream clichés that bombard us every day of our lives: In order to have a good relationship, you have to act a certain way; feminism was responsible for ruining women's love lives; all men are inherently one way while all women are inherently another way; the point of a woman's life is to find The One; and the only thing worth spending your time and energy on is searching for, finding, and getting said One.

I left the bookstore enraged by the way these books, and the mainstream values they regurgitated, were trying to convince single women that there's something wrong with them. And I realized the question that no book addressed—which I now see as one of the biggest of the biggest challenges of our generation—was how savvy, smart, successful, politically conscious women date and find love, on our own terms in a world that is still defined by traditional gender roles, impossible expectations, and archaic relationship models.

According to the sexist manifestos that do exist for women to consume and try to emulate, feminism garnered us privileges that are now ruining our love lives. These so-called experts have a warped and distorted view of feminism, obviously. But as I started to think about the relationship between feminism and, well, relationships, I had to admit that I too found certain limitations. I realized how feminism was being distorted and mischaracterized, but I was also seeing and experiencing where mainstream feminism was coming up short when it came to women's love lives.

Unlike the clichéd writers who hated on feminism, however, and argued that it was too radical, I saw feminism as not radical enough. Popular ideas of feminism have not provided us with enough tools to connect authentically in a world where love and romance have become increasingly commodified. I thought about all the amazing young women I knew who didn't want to date in traditional ways, but who still wanted to date and fall in love. As they sought to negotiate their love lives, many were frustrated by the tension that exists between a sexist dating advice industry and their own strong desire to date. We get so much messaging about what we're doing wrong, and so much advice about what we could be doing better, that when it comes to real-life dating, that messaging has a real, strong, and devastating impact.

I decided it was time for an intervention. I wanted to point out what was wrong with mainstream ideas of romance and dating as seen through movies, books, TV, and the self-help industry. And I wanted to point out where feminism had been misappropriated, and also where feminism had legitimately fallen short. And finally, I wanted to push for a new type of feminism, one that recognizes women's complexities, nuances, and differences and provides us with tools to navigate our personal lives. So I decided to write a feminist book about dating that is both a feminist critique on how we understand dating and a road map to guide us through our feminist dating adventures.

Outdated is about conundrums and confusion; it's about the contradicting messages we get from popular culture, feminism, our social circles, politics, and the romance industry. It's about charting trends in how women and men are talked about in the media; it's about pointing out hypocrisy, and it's about dealing with a world that is still reliant on antiquated ideas of gender.

Love in the Time of Feminism

Throughout this book, I refer to different types of feminism. I have always been reluctant to characterize feminism in waves because it ignores all the many places and spaces where feminism has

happened that have never been labeled as "feminist." But it is important to know what historical moments have impacted which generations and what people are referring to when they use certain terms.
So I present to you the briefest history of feminism ever written:

First-Wave Feminism: Used to describe feminist activism in the
first half of the twentieth century and best known for the work of
the suffragists, a group of women who fought for women's political power and earned us the right to vote. They also worked for
marriage equality and other sexual and reproductive rights.

Second-Wave Feminism: Started in the 1960s and open to debate
as to when exactly it ended, but it's generally agreed upon to be
sometime in the 1980s. Second-wave feminism's main issues included equal pay, reproductive rights (birth control), sex-based
discrimination, and equal rights in marriage. (Second-wave feminists, like first-wavers, engaged themselves in many movements
at once.)

Third-Wave Feminism: Started in the early 1990s and was, in
many ways, a response to feminism being treated as if it were
over. Third-wave feminism brought hope for a new generation of
women that were more diverse and took on issues that were not
just focused on gender, but that extended to other intersections
of identity, such as race, class, sexuality, ability, gender identification, geography, and so on. Third-wave feminism is often associated with riot grrrl culture (which is how I was introduced
to feminism in my suburban New York town—through Bikini Kill
tapes and zines).

Fourth-Wave Feminism: There is some debate as to whether we are in the "fourth wave" yet, or if we are no longer in an era of "waves" and instead just living in a world that has different types of feminism. Some suggest that the fourth wave of feminism is online feminist activism.

Third-wave feminism is often characterized as the wave that's had the most internal divisions, but every wave experienced internal battles. The foundational work of the third wave was introduced during the second wave, generally as an intervention to the second-wave focus on just "women" as a marginalized group. The work of Audre Lorde, Kimberlé Crenshaw, Cherríe Moraga, Gloria Anzaldúa, Chandra Talpade Mohanty, Patricia Hill Collins, and so many others destabilized the assumption that feminism is about only white women. They introduced the idea of intersectionality— that we all exist at the intersection of multiple identities.

Today many types of feminism are acknowledged, both in activism and academia, including transnational feminism, intersectional feminism, environmental feminism, antiracist feminism, transfeminism, cyberfeminism, black feminism, chicana feminism, indigenous feminism, and other identities that centralize feminist ideals but don't claim the title, such as womanism. There is also a lot of debate as to whether feminism has effectively changed the assumption that feminism is about "women," but nonetheless multiple formations of feminism exist and are continually pushing the boundaries of mainstream feminism while creating space for new forms of feminism.

When I refer to mainstream feminism, I'm talking about what is popularly understood in the mainstream media as feminism.

Generally, this is the feminist theory and activism that focused on women as a group of people in need of upliftment, and that fought for workplace equality, for reproductive rights, and for more women in public office. This work is most associated with the previous generation of feminists—Second Wavers—but the work continues today. (One of the limits of characterizing feminism in waves is that we lose the ways in which feminist work has grown organically.)

A feminism based on gender is predicated on a concept called "gender essentialism." Gender essentialism is the belief that your gender (as it is expressed) is tied to your biological sex. It is the logic that says a man is always a "man," with inherent qualities that make him "manly." People have varying viewpoints on the limits and effectiveness of gender essentialism, but that could be another book (and there are many of them). I'm more interested in pushing us to think beyond the belief that you can only be one of two genders, and that if you identify with one, you have to act a certain innate way. I talk about "women" extensively throughout this book, and I'm referring to the people who are targeted by mainstream dating narratives. But I do it with full recognition of the limits of thinking about gender as two innate categories. When I talk about the pressures of femininity and masculinity, I ask that we think past gender as something that is fused to our sex, and that we push ourselves to think about how we understand both biology and socialization, since both have the potential for infinite possibility.

Another concept analogous to gender essentialism and helpful when talking about dating is heteronormativity. Hetero-normativity is a term that was popularized by queer theorist Michael Warner, and builds from Adrienne Rich's concept of "compulsory heterosexuality." Heteronormativity is not just about being straight; it's about all the structures and norms that help privilege monogamous heterosexuality as normal and stigmatizes behavior that deviates from this model. Heteronormativity is more than society telling us that being straight is better; it's also the economic, political, and social structures that reward certain behaviors and make life harder for the people who challenge the status quo. This way of being, which our society wholly endorses, puts people into particular romantic roles based on their gender, replete with assumptions about desire, monogamy, sexual appetite, and chastity.

Gender essentialism and heteronormativity work hand in hand, forcing us into certain roles that we may not want or like, marginalizing "alternative lifestyles," informing popular culture, and shaping policy that promotes traditional behaviors and punishes everything else. Many of us may identify with the gender or sexuality that society tells us corresponds with our biological sex (meaning you are biologically female and identify as a straight woman, or who are biologically male and identify as a straight man). But many of us don't adhere to the traditional definitions and categories; there are biological females who identify as lesbian women, or who identify as men who are attracted to other men and/ or other women; there are biological males who identify as women and are attracted to men and/ or women, or who identify as gay men or bi men or queer men or polyamorous men. Even for those of us whose sexuality and identity happen to adhere to heteronormativity and gender essentialism, there are still moments when we disrupt traditional notions of being a "woman in love," and it is important to create the space to talk about these experiences.

When trying to diagnose the way that romance, sexuality, and gender are represented in the mainstream media, it becomes clear that an intersectional approach gives the most space to understand the complexities we face. But trying to bring intersectional ideas of feminism into the mainstream is not easy work. We are tasked with opening up a dialogue with a public that thinks about identity in a really specific way: you are either a woman or you are black; you are either gay or you are poor; or you are either a (manly) man or a (femme) woman. But most of us fall into multiple camps simultaneously and therefore feel pressures in different ways, have different choices available to us based on the various ways in which we identify, and act on those choices based on who we are. My hope is that an intersectional feminist analysis of dating—initiated through this book—opens up space for us to think creatively about new ways to think about our love lives.

Not Your Typical Dating Book

In light of all the urgent issues facing the world, why would I choose to write a book about something as seemingly frivolous as dating? As Carol Hanisch said, "the personal is political," and nowhere is this truer than in the realm of love. On a very concrete level, our love lives influence our political lives. I firmly believe that if we are not happy and not recognizing what we need in our personal lives, we cannot create the change we want in the communities around us. We are better change-makers, rabble-rousers, organizers, and activists when we are more satisfied, fulfilled, and content. In addition, the fact that so many rights and privileges are contingent on our sexuality and our relationship status tells us that, like it or not, our love lives are political, economic, and social issues—things to be influenced and co-opted. Romance, dating, and love have long been co-opted by corporate and political interest, and we have to fight back, to push for authentic relationships that aren't defined by power, money, and status. Finally, society is changing and we have an opportunity to re-create our love lives in ways never before seen. It is more important than ever to create space for radical love.

For me, love is at the heart of feminism; in this context I'm not just talking about a basic love for humanity and a desire for justice, but also about loving myself in the face of an often-unloving world, about loving the people in my life despite the pain and difficulty of oppression. Love in all its manifestations motivates us; it's what gives us humanity, sentimentality, and compassion. Sometimes, because of this, we don't like to define love; when you are newly "in love" you don't ever want to believe that it might be ultimately tarnished by our other less-than-perfect feelings. After all, being realistic about love makes you a bitter cynic, right? And I certainly don't want to burst anyone's bubble, since love and its anticipation are awesome feelings. But I am here to talk about the ways in which love is socially constructed and affected by our internalized belief systems and external political systems. Love is more than just a chemical or emotional feeling; it is a social and cultural force.

Love doesn't always make a lot of sense. It is one of the hardest emotions and social phenomena to analyze, theorize, or make sociological assumptions about because it is so multifaceted and everywhere.

I think about love in two basic types: Love with a capital "L," which is the broader social and cultural construction of love—the one that our culture, mainstream media, religious institutions, and other structures not only obsess over, but also dictate, measure, and use to inform how we understand love. And then there's love with a little "l," which is the love we feel interpersonally (the love we feel for lovers, family members, and friends) and impersonally (the love we feel toward life, humanity, earth, hobbies, and work).

Often our interpersonal love (little "l" love) is dictated by expectations being fed to us by the big "L" Love. The way love manifests is specific to our lived experience and how love has played out in our lives, which runs the spectrum from denial of love to codependence to healthy, loving families. We all carry with us the information of how we have received, known, and acted on love.

And because love is so pervasive, so necessary, and so fundamental to society, many institutions have rituals moderating, controlling, and denying things that happen within its purview. Some common ones all of us can recognize include wedding rituals; legislation that defines whom you can marry or have sex with; politics used to maintain the definition of marriage as being between a man and a woman; immigration policies that keep inter/ transnational lovers apart; healthcare access based on your marital status; or the denial of domestic violence within the sanctity of marriage. These are just a few ways that love is manipulated by capital "L" Love to deny or give access to certain rights. Oftentimes beliefs and policies like these function as obstacles to love. As a result, love can end up being fraught with pain, fear, jealousy, obsession, power, and control. And still, despite all these side effects, people strive for love, endlessly.

This book doesn't have all the answers, nor does it guarantee that you will find happiness once you've finished reading. This is not a guide on how to meet the man of your dreams or how to figure out the secret held under lock and key to fulfill your greatest romantic desires (well, maybe it is). I'm not going to shame you like other dating book authors do. And I'm not going to yell at you for what you did wrong or tell you why you deserve what you have gotten when it comes to love.

Every chapter in this book does one of three things: (1) calls into question sexist narratives in mainstream dating advice; (2) points out the limits of both pop-feminism and mainstream feminism; and (3) pushes for deeper analysis and rethinking of these issues through a more radical sense of feminism.

In Chapter 1, we'll look at how biology has been used to justify how men and women experience love differently and how it has also been used as evidence for how feminism ruined romance. This chapter makes a case for how feminism has done the exact opposite and has actually helped romance.

Chapter 2 takes on the politics of representation and how the choices, roles, and behaviors of our political leaders force us into limited options for our relationships. We'll look at how nationalist ideas of womanhood limit our choices when it comes to how we experience being women, and how the gay marriage debate has highlighted the shortcomings of a society founded on heteronormativity.

Chapter 3 critiques the current romantic fairytales our society is obsessed with and how they play out in our day-to-day dating situations, informing our ideas about our bodies and ourselves.

In Chapter 4, we'll consider the ways in which mainstream dating advice is hurting our dating lives by manipulating our emotions, playing into our gender differences, and failing to recognize the biggest reason dating is so difficult: Society is still sexist.

In Chapter 5, we'll discuss the feminist idea of the "single gal" about town and how current lore has it that the single gal is the ultimate feminist goal. And yet, structurally, little has changed in society to support single women. We'll also dissect popular narratives about single life and how they have privileged a certain kind of single lady.

In Chapter 6, popular concepts of masculinity are explored. Men aren't getting off easy here at all; messaging and dating advice hurt them, too. Negative messaging about what it means to be a "man" today has led to a plethora of toxic side effects when it comes to dating.

In Chapter 7, we'll discuss what happens when we try to apply our feminism to our dating lives.

Chapter 8 covers "hookup culture" and casual sex as legitimate alternatives to heteronormativity. We'll also talk about how dominant ideas about women and sex have hurt our ways of having authentic pleasurable sexual experiences.

And finally, Chapter 9 presents creative ways to use feminism in our love lives, to push for not only the relationships we want, but also for the romantic communities we want to cultivate.

FEMINISM
DIDN'T RUIN DATING,

DATiNG ruined DATING

I know this is an unpopular thing to say, but feminism has completely fucked up my love life. To be fair, it's not feminism, exactly—after all, "feminism" never published a dating manual—but what I considered to be "the feminist way of doing things" certainly didn't help. It's not that I would give back the gains of feminism for anything. Believe me, I wouldn't. It's just that I wish I hadn't tried to apply what I believed to be "feminist ideals" to dating.

—Lori Gottlieb, *Marry Him*

{ CHAPTER ONE } The mainstream media has an unhealthy obsession with women's love lives. You would be hard pressed to open a newspaper or magazine or even to find a television channel that doesn't highlight women's marital status, drone on about the death of romance or the fall of masculinity, or bemoan the shortage of single eligible men.

Toxic media myths about women and love are ruining our love lives. Why? They assume that all women want to find Prince Charming, and worse, that we are too independent for our own good. They tell us we are "fat." They tell us that earning too much money will emasculate the men in our lives. They tell us that our college educations are boner-killers. And most damagingly, they tell us we shouldn't be who we have fought long and hard to become.

Similar to Gottlieb's assertion, two of the most nefarious and popular memes readily available today about love and romance are that feminism ruined romance and that men and women are inherently different when it comes to love and sex. As women we are trapped between two stories: popular feminism telling us we don't need a man and mainstream dating advice telling us we have to play into gender stereotypes to find and meet the man of our dreams. Most of us just want to date, and if you're honest with yourself you know that you either do or don't always want to do it like everyone is telling you you should.

It's Not You, It's Everything Else

Everyone from self-proclaimed feminist dating advice gurus to conservative religious wingnuts like to deride feminism for ruining romance. In the same vein as Gottlieb, in early 2011, two relationship "experts," Samantha Brett and Donna Sozio, wrote in their self-professed groundbreaking book, *The Man Whisperer*, "While women were achieving what they wanted in their careers, many made the mistake of instantly thinking that insisting on equality was also the way to get what they wanted in their romantic lives." Brett and Sozio, both feminist-identified, conclude that feminism taught us to want everything like a "man," but insist that this has hurt us in our dating lives because to catch a man (or to be a man whisperer), we have to be in touch with our more feminine qualities (i.e., being passive, demure, nonthreatening, and, of course, waiting to be caught). Apparently, Victorian-era ideas of romance are alive and thriving.[1]

I can give them credit for having tapped into one major problem: applying popular assumptions about feminism to your dating life can be challenging (more on that later). But feminism is not the culprit here. Rather, it's the narrow way we understand gender and the limited options we have when it comes to how we're supposed to be in a relationship. In trying to give refreshing new advice, people like Brett, Sozio, and Gottlieb manage to fall right into the myopic antifeminist tradition of contemporary dating advice that tells women: Freedom and equality have been great for us, but it's killed our love lives.

The enemy to romance today is always feminism, but nobody wants to talk about the greater pressures we face in the "search" for love. When it comes to dating, society tells us that to be happy we have to be in one specific type of relationship—a straight, heterosexual, monogamous one. We are constantly bombarded with messages about whom we should date, how we should love, and why we should marry. These messages are almost impossible not to internalize, and doing so has a devastating impact on how we feel about ourselves, and the way we date and seek happiness.

The difference between what most of us *have* and what we're taught to *want* leads to cognitive dissonance that continually results in feelings of alienation, loneliness, and general unhappiness (and sometimes bitterness). After all, if you are someone who hasn't found The One, or if you don't define yourself based on your romantic relationships, finding happiness can take a lot more work, because it means figuring out what you want for yourself while dealing with messages coming at you from all over the place from people who claim to know what is best for you.

The heteronormative nature of our society means we grow up pursuing a certain romantic ideal (despite its many flaws) that highlights what you don't have while "othering" lifestyles that don't adhere to that ideal. Many of us want to be in relationships, want to date and find love, and yet we're unconsciously adhering to that ideal that's been hammered into our heads since we were kids. It takes a lot of awareness to start to figure out that things might not be as they seem. If dating starts to feel pressured, or you feel like you're having to live up to a certain way of being in relationship, you've undoubtedly bought into the idea that you're supposed to be dating and finding love in a certain way. This was true for me, so much so that I started feeling like I somehow had a problem, that I wasn't good enough, and that maybe if I tried harder the love of my life would show up on my proverbial doorstep.

Well, I didn't have a problem—and neither do you. We feel this way because there is no legitimate space for those of us who are not in a Serious Monogamous Relationship. As women, if we have not successfully found a serious, long-term, heterosexual relationship that is leading to marriage, we are left in a post-feminist disaster area where romantic dreams go to die, cat ladies are in abundance, and happiness is something we don't deserve.

Because we are taught that something is wrong with us when our romantic endeavors are failing, we can face undue pressure to hold our relationships together even when they're not working. Regardless of the kind of relationship you might want to be in, there is an expectation that you have a vested interest in keeping your current relationship alive. You have a lot to lose if your relationship is not working out, or if you are not dating, or worse, if you are single because you want to be (blasphemy!).

Yet, increasingly more and more people are choosing unconventional paths. Casual relationships, cohabitation, non-monogamy, same-sex relationships, quirkyalones, single moms, single dads, cohabiting co-parents, and disenchanted-single-straight-leaning-and-annoyed (okay, I made that one up) have become more common choices where relationships are concerned. And yet, despite the fact that we're seeing alternative choices as more legitimate options, there is still a tremendous amount of pressure to fit into a "normal" relationship mold.

Mainstream dating advice claims that feminism ruined our love lives, but this is a fallacy. What's missing from this proclamation is that what's put into the mainstream and considered "feminist" is often an appropriated version of feminism that rests on ideas such as: "I don't need a man to be successful" and "I can do anything he can do (better)." The idea that women can do anything men can do, while invaluable in some ways, is not all there is to feminism. The notion that it is has not only hurt public ideas of feminism, but it's given space for people like Sarah Palin to call themselves feminists, regardless of how antifeminist their views are, just because they are women doing things traditionally done by men. It has allowed Ariel Levy to blame feminism for "raunch culture" and demand that it's feminism's fault that young women are comfortable having sex "like men." Pop-feminism has moved our focus to individual choices as opposed to larger structural problems (such as sexualization of girls in the media—a much more plausible cause for supposed "raunch" culture than feminism). One very effective feminist tool in distorting feminism was shifting the public perception of feminism from a vibrant and rich social movement to minimizing it to the individual choices women make.

According to mainstream media, feminism is anything you want it to be; you use it when you need it, irrelevant of how many contradictions it might present. This co-opted and distorted representation of feminism, while loosely based on some of the ideals mainstream feminism has stood for, is continually referred to in any writing on dating, love, and romance. This problematically and systematically ignores the very real space feminists have made for how we talk about sexuality, romance, love, and dating.

While the media, including those who put forth mainstream dating advice, blames feminism for everything from promiscuity to the perceived loss of family values, the feminist movement (as in the actual movement that started petitions, marched for women's lives, and created change in sexist policies) has been invaluable in improving public dialogue around popular ideas about love, relationships, gender, and motherhood. And while feminists are often ridiculed for being "antisex" and "antiromance," without their work we wouldn't even be talking about the pressures we feel in our romantic lives, nor would we have the romantic and sexual options we do (as limited and myopic as those options continue to be). If it weren't for Betty Friedan questioning married life (albeit limited to a certain class of women) or Gloria Steinem's critique of marriage (even though her views ultimately changed as the institution did), we would not even have a language to talk about the pressures we face to love and date a certain way.

Furthermore, there is evidence to suggest that feminism actually makes women and men happier individuals, and therefore happier in their love lives. In 2007, two researchers at Rutgers interviewed 242 undergraduates and 289 older adults to find out what their views on feminism were and what their relationship status was. They found that having a feminist partner made the relationship healthier, that men in relationships with feminists were more sexually satisfied, and that feminist women were more likely to be in relationships than were nonfeminist women. This study found the conventional wisdom that feminism and romance are opposing forces to be false.[2, 3]

All this said, it can be difficult to apply mainstream ideas of feminism to our love lives. It is one thing to lobby for policy change, head an organization, fight for workplace equality, or point out the drawbacks of traditional relationships. How we use feminism in our interpersonal or romantic lives, however, is a whole different battle.

Call Me Anything, But Don't Call Me That Girl

The disconnect between theory and practice is at the heart of much of the dissonance young women experience when it comes to using feminism to navigate their romantic lives. For example, have you ever let the guy you're dating off the hook for something he did that upset you because you were invested in being the "casual, strong, independent, not needy" girl? You are not alone. These are values championed by feminists everywhere, and yet there are instances where we betray ourselves for the sake of emulating qualities we value. When this happens, you are bumping up against something a lot of women struggle with: how to reconcile sexist ideas of what it means to be a woman in a relationship with our own understanding of what it means to be adhering to feminist values.

I remember telling my best friend for the umpteenth time that it was okay, despite a series of neglectful moves on behalf of her then "almost sorta maybe" boyfriend, to still love him and be with him. After all, I rationalized, she didn't want a relationship in the traditional sense, so this "here today, gone tomorrow" relationship seemed just fine. The truth was that there was nothing fine about it. Nothing about feeling unsatisfied, unhappy, neglected, or insecure is ever fine. But I felt—and many of my friends agreed—that she (and all of us by extension) should be fine with a relationship that (sort of) incorporated our values of independence and feminism. We call this the "Great Sacrifice" of dating as feminists, meaning that we accept things that are "good enough" in the service of our larger political ideals. Unfortunately, in practice this often means settling for someone who isn't right in the name of being calm, cool, and "happy."

We were inadvertently trying to avoid being a sexist stereotype: the Desperate Girl. Author/doctor and self-proclaimed dating advice guru Travis Stork, author of *Don't Be That Girl* (one of the most offensive books I've ever stumbled across) dedicates a chapter to Desperate Girl in his misogynist guidebook to the various kinds of girl you "shouldn't" be. In addition to Desperate Girl are Lonely Girl, Bitter Girl, Career Girl, Drama Queen Girl, and others, complete with descriptions of how you can spot and label these "girls" yourself. Desperate Girl is needy, calls too often, and wants to know when you are going to call and how often she can see you. In other words, you're *that girl* if you have a personality or any expectations out of a relationship.[4]

Unfortunately, the most feminist of us has so internalized the sexist condemnation of the Desperate Girl that we will do anything we can—including betraying our feelings and instincts—to not be her. Needy, desperate, and nagging are all labels slapped on women when they have needs or demands in a relationship, and it's based on sexist and retrograde ideas that women are inherently more emotional and therefore must always be managed by men. The assumption is that women always want more and that men always want less. No modern feminist woman wants to be Desperate Girl, or any of the "girls" in Stork's book for that matter. These unfair and sexist characterizations encourage men to be dismissive of women's needs while simultaneously silencing women by shaming them with stereotypical examples of how women act in relationships.

In my own relationships, rather than express that I was frustrated or unhappy, I sometimes felt the right thing to do was to act more "feminist" to fight being cast as Desperate Girl. I felt I had too much to lose, both in terms of feminist credibility and in my own understanding of my relationship as "unconventional."

Turns out, pretending you are happy in a relationship that is actually making you unhappy is exhausting. Some people do it for a lifetime, until it becomes second nature; others do it because they think they have no other options; still others do it because they're afraid to show their true selves and what they really want; and finally there are those who do it because they are afraid to be alone. And given that so many people are tragically inept when it comes to healthy communication, negotiating relationships that don't make us happy is an ongoing battle.

When I was in my twenties (around the time I told my friend it was a good idea to stay in her bad relationship), I struggled with the fact that the feminism I'd been adhering to was no longer working for me. I needed more options. The media paints feminism as either the "bra-burning shoulder pad set," or the Camille Paglia/Katie Roiphe/Lori Gottlieb "I hate feminists even though I am one" set. The lack of representation of young, diverse feminists talking candidly about how they are navigating their romantic lives today has led countless young women to a place of feeling alienated by feminism. The reasons for this are obvious: We want to date and find love, we just don't want to do it the way the world around us is telling us we should. And being a "man whisperer" is not a legitimate alternative.

In my mid-twenties, when I got more involved in feminist circles, and especially when I started writing for *Feministing*, it was hard for me to reconcile what I perceived to be feminist behaviors—keeping things really casual, or being cool with not hearing from my partner, or agreeing to be open—with the fact that I was unhappy in my dating life. I had entered a space where things felt unsafe and suddenly I didn't know how to articulate what was going on for me without risking looking less independent, or somehow less feminist. I wanted to be in a happy, healthy, non-codependent relationship, but I didn't know how to go about it with the models I had in front of me.

After my last breakup, I finally got it. It wasn't feminism that was hurting my love life, it wasn't that I had too many needs, and it wasn't that women had changed too much; it was that society had not changed *enough*. The world around me still expected me to be in a certain kind of relationship and to go through all the motions of getting that ideal relationship. Meanwhile, I was stuck, vacillating between social expectations (which in my case were compounded by having been brought up in the South Asian community), what I understood to be feminist romantic ideals, and what I wanted for myself. I knew I didn't want to be in a traditional relationship, but I wanted more accountability in my relationships.

And when I took a look around, I was astounded by how outdated the conversation we are still having about dating really is. The "man whisperers" of the world seemed to dominate popular ideas about feminism and romance, all of which rely on traditional ideas of gender and don't take into account how people today are dating and/or negotiating our relationships.

Particularly frustrating was the assumption that the key to happiness for women was through a conventional or traditional relationship. Sure, they can and do lead to happiness, but sometimes they don't. The expectation that conventional relationships are the key to happiness puts pressure on women to feel like they have to be in a relationship instead of highlighting other accomplishments and supporting other relationships (like friendships!). And it ignores that roles for women have changed profoundly, and that doing what is expected of us doesn't always make us happy.

Some women, of course, have recognized this, as many of us are openly defining our relationships by a different set of standards that don't include "Where is this going?" but rather

"Is this a nice person and is this relationship stable?" Or, as a friend quoted to me, "Reliability is the new fine!" So while it's always been true that relationships are easier and feel better when a lot of people support them, that doesn't make a conventional, easy-to-explain relationship the right or only option.

These new markers of successful relationships indicate that whatever stability is supposed to come with traditional relationships is no longer the driving force behind successful or long-term relationships. And while plenty of women want that stability without the tradition, for those who don't, the social expectation to get married is near impossible to ignore. Thus, our ability to be in a relationship that stands apart from tradition *and* feels good falls short because of the lack of emotional, social, political, and economic structures to support it.

As anyone who's ever fought for a social cause knows, there's a difference between what you believe and how what you believe gets played out in your life. Idealistic values that are based in political ideologies, such as labor politics, animal rights, and anti-capitalist movements, are often difficult to align with 100 percent because it's difficult to live in a world that's thriving on the very things we are fighting against. Feminism is no different. Applying what we understand feminism to be to our personal lives leaves a lot of room for error. When the answers to our basic questions about how to get emotional accountability from men without being cast as "needy," or how to balance a desire for a relationship in a world that demands you act a certain way to meet a man, are met with, *Well, you shouldn't be a feminist in your romantic endeavors anyway*, you start to believe you can't successfully be a feminist behind closed doors.

Not having solid feminist relationship models to help us navigate personal relationships in a patriarchal world leaves us high and dry. We live in a culture that's reluctant to let go of a model of romance that assumes unequal power between men and women. And while feminism left fertile ground for re-invention, it also allowed for the propagation of unequal power relations—and it happened almost without us even noticing. Saying you "don't need a man" didn't go far enough, because many of us *are* dating men and the power differentials in those relationships still go unchecked. I would argue that we start to believe that the power imbalance is just something we have to put up with if we want to date.

This may sound like a case against feminism, but it's exactly the opposite. It's a call to think creatively about how to apply our feminism to our personal lives and how to push against institutional powers that force us to believe that our destiny is a specific type of relationship. Feminism has given young women the ability to recognize the ways in which patriarchy functions in our love lives and our romantic lives; it's also opened our eyes to just how much marketing and messaging affect how we date.

The media and antifeminist response to women feeling disenchanted with our love lives has been to co-opt what's important to us and proclaim that it's feminism that's ruining our love lives. But this isn't the case. In fact, feminism exists to make our love lives better, to help us make more informed and confident choices, and to push for a world that is more accepting of alternative relationship models. The time has come for us to put the theory into action.

Retrograde Gender Roles: The Gift That Keeps on Giving

The theme that women's independence has ruined romance is not just peddled by social critics and relationship advice "gurus." In the last few years there has been an onslaught of studies that claim gender differences between men and women are to blame for both sexes being so unhappy in their relationships. The debate over how much of what we desire in love and romance is "natural" versus how much of it is learned has been going on for decades. As someone who studies how power relations work in gender and society, my observations are limited to critiques of methodology as opposed to the scientific findings themselves. However, it's clear that the ever-popular pseudoscience of love bases its findings on an overreliance on gender being essential when it comes to love.

John Gray's hugely popular *Men Are from Mars, Women Are from Venus* was the pinnacle of gender essentialism in the 1990s. He offered a lively, "no-bull" diagnosis of what he believed men and women really wanted out of relationships and gave us a new and particularly harmful vocabulary for expressing gender difference in relationships. While his book is (out)dated now, the ideas he put forward reverberate in contemporary dating books. Throughout the mountains of dating books I surveyed, there was one consistent theme: retrograde gender roles are back and continue to inform the way romance is written about, researched, and characterized.

This bizarre fetishization of gender essentialism is notable not just for sociopolitical and cultural reasons, but also because it completely overlooks the ways in which real people are partnering. As previously mentioned, cohabitation has become more popular than ever before; unmarried people head more house-holds than ever and almost half the adult population in the United States is unmarried. As of 2005, 4.85 million couples were cohabitating.[5] As of 2008, the U.S. Census Bureau American Community Survey (ACS) reported that 104 million Americans over eighteen were unmarried, which is approximately 45 percent of the adult population. The ACS also reported in 2007 that unmarried people headed 51 million households in the United States. And in 2005, unmarried households became the majority of U.S. households.[6] In one of the most comprehensive studies done on women and girls since the '60s (commissioned by the Obama administration in 2011), the U.S. Department of Commerce Economics and Statistics Administration found that both men and women are marrying five years later on average than they were in 1950.[7]

Gender variance, transgender identities, queer identities, and gender nonconformity, despite frequently being marginalized, are increasingly visible identities—and they're a vocal minority when it comes to their sexual and relationship rights, too. Aside from the fact that they're heading up nontraditional households quite successfully, their very existence shows us that a reliance on gender essentialism is a flawed framework for understanding love, romance, and relationships. The work of butch, femme, queer, transgender and feminist activists, researchers, and theoreticians, while not perfect and often competing, has pushed the boundaries of how we understand the gender binary, proving that across history, geography, and culture, gender is varied. Their work has shown that a reliance on a gender essentialist framework is not just problematic—it is false and irresponsible.

More often than not, the heavily quoted research on gender and dating that the media loves to hang onto gets debunked—only the media gives the rebuttal far less attention. In *Same Difference,* authors Rosalind Barnett and Caryl Rivers tracked some of the leading research on gender difference and romance (among other areas) to find that, time and time again, it was not biological gender differences that caused variation in behaviors between men and women, but rather the way that power played out between them. In responding to the work of David Buss, a leading evolutionary psychologist whose work concluded that men are always attracted to younger women and women are attracted to older breadwinners, Barnett and Rivers, citing the work of two researchers who reanalyzed Buss's data after looking at trends in women's equality, wrote that as "gender equality in society increased, women expressed less preference for older men with greater earning potential, and men expressed less preference for younger women with domestic skills."[8] Despite this evidence suggesting Buss's data may be flawed, his work is heavily cited by popular evolutionary psychologists who want to prove that it is somehow natural for men to be attracted to younger women and for women to be attracted to richer men. But as it turns out, it's social circumstances that impact whom we desire romantically as much as economic ones.

Similarly, in *Delusions of Gender,* Cordelia Fine takes issue with faux scientists' poorly constructed experiments, which too often make sweeping generalizations about gender difference. What she terms "neurosexism" has almost become a field of study. Fine looks at how gender is codified into our psyche through our associative memory—something so powerful we may not even realize how we make choices based on it. She writes, "[T]he principle behind learning in associative memory is simple: as its name suggests, what is picked up are associations in the environment. Place a woman behind almost every vacuum cleaner being pushed around a carpet and, by Jove, associative memory will pick up the pattern."[9] Similar kinds of learned associations about how gender dynamics should function in our romantic lives abound, whether it be through images of women in wedding dresses, prince and princess fairytales, or knights in shining armor rescuing damsels in distress. Cultural romantic fairytales and the modern ways they play out are continually reinforced in movies, books, pictures, magazines, and television.

There is overwhelming evidence to support that gender is constructed and that gender essentialism and the science that promotes it are problematic. Articles and studies that deal with the science of romance give too little credence to social construction and opt for "conventional" wisdom to frame oftentimes faulty or unsubstantiated findings. In recent years, a number of studies have concluded that women respond to situations one way and men another—and biology and evolution are used to support these claims. Men are natural hunters and aggressors and women are passive objects to be possessed, cared for, and displayed. The "natural" conclusion here is that independent women with brains and careers are not good candidates for relationships. And thus the expectation is that women must sacrifice their lives—settling, adapting more passive roles—or they will not find relationships.

This idea of gender difference also extends to the analysis of how women have sex versus how men have sex; how women respond to casual sexual encounters versus how men do; and, of course, what women want out of romantic relationships versus what men do. The greatest perpetrators of the myth "women can't have casual sex" are the evolutionary psychologists, faux scientists, and religious wingnuts.

The queen of love and evolutionary psychology, Helen Fisher, asserts that biological gender is responsible for differences in how men and women behave when it comes to love. In her book, *Why We Love*, Fisher looks at a series of brain scans and concludes that women and men not only are inherently different in their biological makeup, but also in the way they think, which is why they behave so differently in relationships. This, she claims, is what leads to a lot of the miscommunications between the sexes. She asserts tired stereotypes, like women like to talk more, think more long-term, and lead with emotion, whereas men express their love through action. And while she recognizes the role of "nurture," she all but ignores it in the service of her greater "scientifically" proven belief that sex difference accounts for the supposedly "different" ways that men and women behave when it comes to love.[10]

What I'm most taken aback by in Fisher's work is her complete denial of gender variation. Her research has been challenged by others, including a team at the University of Arizona that found that the discrepancy between how much men and women talk is not as large as previous social scientists have found it to be.[11] Also, the bulk of Fisher's brain scans are done through fMRI brain scans, something Cordelia Fine also took to task in *Delusions of Gender*, writing, "Inferring a psychological state from brain activity . . . is known as reverse inference, and as any neuroimager will tell you, it is fraught with peril."[12] This is not to say that there is no difference between how someone socialized as a man versus someone socialized as a woman responds to romance or falling in love. However, it's critical that we start to ask for accountability when ideas are promoted as having been scientifically proven, when really they're inferences based on observations. The gap between observable data and many conclusions about how men and women act with regard to romance is too large to draw mass generalizations from.

Fisher's hypothesis is compelling and tempting to propagate because it gives us an easy way to justify social conventions that can be difficult to stand up to. It's easier to believe that men and women are inherently different when it comes to love than to do the difficult work of pushing against the grain and suggesting that romance is a socially constructed fantasy. Falling into this status quo way of thinking—that men behave one way and women another—gives men the privilege and power to make the first move, ask you out, propose, and support you. It also imposes limitations on them in that it lets them off the hook where expressing their emotions is concerned (or worse yet, it chastises them for it).

The endless obsession with how women are going to die alone because they have brains, careers, and casual sex has been the new "trend" for a while. Fisher is actually one of the more grounded authors out there (and actually a scientist and therefore not using her findings to support a religious agenda—as others have). The worst offenders are "pop culture" psychologists whose findings are often concocted to look like this: Mix one part college student sample, a few scattered inconsistent findings based on loosely correlated "evidence," sweeping generalizations that reinforce female anxiety around mating, some incorrect data on oxytocin, and some slut-shaming for good measure.

Mark Regnerus and sociologist Jeremy Uecker are examples of this type of "relationship expert." Their book, *Premarital Sex in America: How Young Americans Meet, Mate, and Think about Marrying,* claims to understand the sexual behavior of young people through a series of interviews with college students. They assert that women who have casual sex in college will regret it later in life when they are trying to be in a serious relationship. It is important to note that Regnerus made his mark when he published an article that told women to get married early to avoid premarital sex—so we kind of already know where he is coming from.[13, 14]

Regnerus's key conclusion is that men have the upper hand when it comes to sex. This is not because women are judged based on their promiscuity or lack thereof in a way that men rarely are, or because men face pressure to have casual sex and deny their romantic feelings for relationships. (Or because when you are a woman between the ages of eighteen and twenty-three—the age of the subjects—male attention and the desire to be in a relationship impact your self-esteem more deeply than, say, when you are a thirtysomething.) No, no, men have the upper hand in sex and dating because women have too much freedom, sex, and education.

Regnerus and Uecker found that college-aged women don't feel they need men for financial independence and can have casual sex as they please. The problem, they conclude, comes later, when these women decide they want to be in serious relationships and there are so many other slutty, trampy women who are willing to have sex without commitment that it ultimately leaves these women without a man who will be willing to commit to them. Because, I mean, who cares about men's feelings anyway, right? They seem to be missing the point that when you are college-aged you're generally not self-supporting or paying all your own bills. You're still figuring out what you want in life, out of your career, and out of your relationships. And check out the circular slut-shaming: Women are being blamed for other women being promiscuous as though it is a zero-sum game and the problem is other women having sex rather than men's sexual choices. And men, well, they are just men, of course! Forget all the ones who actually do want long-term, fulfilling relationships.

And despite how fun and easy it is to poke holes in these kinds of arguments, we can't entirely write off biological *or* social differences between the sexes. There is truth to biological essentialism, and there is truth to the idea that gender is learned. The problem is that biological essentialism is often exaggerated and/or based on questionable data and a whole lot of guessing. In her book, *Whipping Girl*, Julia Serano writes that socialization does not inherently produce gender difference but, "it seems to me more accurate to say that in many cases socialization acts to exaggerate biological gender differences that already exist . . . "[15] Biology can be about endless and infinite possibility, but when squeezed through the limiting framework of sexism, it generally functions to harm how we think, feel, and act in our romantic endeavors.

Sadly, the types of studies I mention here have come to dominate popular culture writing on the science of love. Sexist and gendered assumptions about how people date and mate are taken as truth and inspire article after article that shame women about their dating and love lives and insist that men are just "men," so our best bet, as women, is to appease them.

The belief that gender is a static binary with innate qualities has impacted entire industries—not just the romance industry, but magazines, movies, mainstream media, fiction, and self-help, not to mention the academic fields of psychology, sociology, and anthropology. But the main problem appears to be that women's independence has led to a "condition" where we don't *need* to date anymore; we only do it if we want to. This unwillingness to settle, to want to be romantically self-determined and not give your vagina up to every "nice guy" you meet, has the mainstream media, relationship experts, and faux scientists up in arms, scrambling to find scientific, social, and political reasons to keep us buying into a romantic story that is tragically outdated.

SEARCHING
FOR CITIZENSHIP IN
the State of Love

I still think it's important for people to have a sharp, ongoing critique of marriage in patriarchal society—because once you marry within a society that remains patriarchal, no matter how alternative you want to be within your unit, there is still a culture outside you that will impose many, many values on you whether you want them to or not.

—bell hooks

{ CHAPTER TWO } They stole my crayons and called me smelly Indian girl. They wouldn't play with me. They made fun of the way my name sounded. They didn't ask me to be their prom date. *They were my peers from grade school to high school and they made my life a living hell.*

Growing up in a predominantly working/middle-class Irish and Italian neighborhood in the suburbs of New York City with few other South Asians not only made me racially and ethnically different, but also an outcast. From as far back as I can remember, I didn't fit in. As I got older, I started to become self-conscious of being different: I looked different, spoke different, and smelled different (sounds like such a cliché). Like many out-of-the-ordinary youth growing up in places that strive for homogeneity, I learned early to be embarrassed of who I was.

Unfortunately, I never really found comfort with the South Asian community I grew up around. I didn't appreciate the expectations my parents and their friends had for me, I wasn't a particularly good student, and I had no foreseeable future as a doctor, lawyer, or engineer. My parents were supportive, as long as I was doing *something;* but they, along with their friends, had very specific ideas about life, love, and the pursuit of happiness. The pressure to get married and be a certain way *felt* very serious to my teenage punk rock sensibilities. Being a "good" Indian girl was diametrically opposed to what I wanted to be, which was, of course, cool. (You remember being a teenager.)

When faced with a situation like this, you can assimilate or rebel, and you can guess which way I went. I became part of a tribe of outcasts who intentionally stood out from the rest of the "normal" kids. By the time we got to high school, we were the freaks, geeks, nerds, dorks, and weirdos. Being a group of gender-questioning, antiestablishment, alternative music listening (yes, Rage Against the Machine happened when I was in high school) misfits kept our dating prospects limited (shocking, I know). But it wasn't just people's ignorance that kept my friends and me from being considered desirable in the small-minded dating pool of my tiny Northern Westchester high school; it was our refusal to accept the mandatory heterosexuality. I was acutely aware, even back then, that my self-esteem and identity were supposed to be validated by male attention. Refusing to participate in the popularity Olympics meant that my friends and I were either ignored or chastised.

As a young feminist, my identity was more solidly locked in rebelling against the expected gender roles I was supposed to live up to than seeking male attention. I didn't have a boyfriend and I believed that making yourself desirable for a man was weak. I was the quintessential mid-'90s punk rock feminist riot grrrl. And yet, I was, in fact, completely boy crazy. Under the surface of my fuck-you look—shaving off most of my hair and dying it purple, wearing all black, having fifteen ear piercings, and wearing lots of black eye makeup—was a desire to fit in and get male attention. On one level I had internalized the belief that it wasn't possible because I had always been different and hadn't been noticed by boys; and on another level, the lack of male attention gave me the opportunity to realize how fundamentally flawed it is that a woman would act a certain way to fit in and get male attention. And so I chose to build my identity around the rejection of this expectation.

Anyone who knows a teenager can attest to the fact that rebellion is a normal reaction when you feel powerless. Fundamental to being an American female is the desire to fit in, get attention from certain guys, and perform a certain type of femininity. I never could be and ultimately never wanted to be the American dream of femininity.

Being a South Asian geek obsessed with subculture and having a flair for disaffected behavior didn't make me different from my peers. For me it was my race, ethnicity, and the fact that the misfits I ran with largely identified as queer that made me different. But there are any number of things that make us different beyond our race, sexual orientation, or musical choices. Many young people feel alienated in high school because of who they are, whether that's because they're questioning their sexuality, or they're the only Asian kid in their all-white high school, or just because they're a teenager and it's a confusing and difficult time.

Most youth struggle with the pressures of fitting in, but it gets serious when young people are teased, chastised, or bullied for being different. I was lucky; I had a tight-knit group of friends that fostered a strong sense of belonging and deterred *most* bullying—but many young people aren't so lucky.

The issue of young people questioning their romantic choices and trying to define themselves outside of the norm has become a more salient point in the last few years as gay and transgender bullying has been thrust into the national spotlight after a series of suicides that finally captured the attention of the media. Defying normative and ascribed gender and sexuality roles makes you a target of ridicule, public shaming, and violence. Being able to be who you are, especially as a gay or trans young person, is about more than fitting in; it is a matter of feeling respected for who you are and being afforded the same rights as your peers. The lessons we learn when we're young about the appropriate ways to express our sexuality and gender is informed by a larger story about romance that's pushed along by history, nostalgia, and politics. Anxieties about belonging don't come from high school, but from the world around us.

Mandatory Heterosexuality and the Gotcha Game

Heterosexual coupling, whether through dating or marriage, is considered a fundamental tenet of American society. Heterosexual monogamy is normalized not just through practice, but also through (pseudo) science (as we saw in Chapter 1), corporate interest (which we'll cover in Chapter 3), policy, public expectation, shaming, and ritual. One step beyond normalization is compulsory heterosexuality, which is on display most notably among our political figures and religious leaders—regardless of what their actual affiliations and sexual compulsions might be.

Beyond the expectation that our politicians be heterosexual is the expectation they carry forward on our behalf that heterosexuality be mandatory for the populace too—even though everyone knows this doesn't work. After so many gay sex scandals and divorces, you would think they would let it go; but no, politicians continually push their own perfect image of what the American public has been taught they're supposed to want: that their representatives be straight, happily married, and monogamous. And yet, consider the sex scandals of the last few decades that have become a mainstay of political coverage: Bill Clinton, Eliot Spitzer, Mark Sanford, John Ensign, John Edwards, Larry Craig, David Vitter, James McGreevey, Robert Livingston, and Newt Gingrich, to name a few, have either admitted to or been "caught" having extramarital affairs, both gay and straight.

Almost all of these politicians acted out in either misogynistic or homophobic ways, too. John Ensign, who ardently criticized Bill Clinton's extramarital transgressions and was a fierce advocate of banning same-sex marriage, had an affair with the wife of one of his top aides (talk about the sanctity of marriage!). Larry Craig, who ultimately never admitted to his crime, despite pleading guilty, had a lifetime of antigay politics and legislation behind him when he was arrested for "lewd conduct" toward another man in the bathroom at the Minneapolis-St. Paul International Airport. David Vitter, another advocate of banning same-sex marriage, was a client of the DC Madam (a much stronger way to undermine your marriage than supporting the notion that two men you don't even know can get married, if you ask me). Many of the politicians I named above heralded themselves on family values; they supported anti-sex work policy and homophobic legislation, yet were caught in extramarital affairs or same-sex relations.

These incidents suggest that mandatory heterosexuality is a socially constructed myth, so much so that even its greatest proponents can't effectively participate in it. This is not about supporting the rights of powerful white men who think they're invincible to explore their sexuality (I mean, someone should take up that cause I guess, but not me), but rather to shine light on the reality that as long as there is a political imperative for how relationships should be, the more mandatory that model becomes.

The hypocrisy we see among politicians seems to know no end. We have politicians who run on a platform of family values who cheat on their wives and those who spew antigay rhetoric and are later caught in a homosexual act behind closed doors. And while it may seem like exposing their hypocrisy is the right and fair thing to do, the game of "gotcha" often ends up doing the opposite of what it intends (exposing hypocrisy) and instead reconsolidates the belief that being gay is something to be ashamed of. Ann Friedman of *The American Prospect* opined, "One could argue that there are political gains to be won by outing, especially if sufficiently shamed antigay politicians resign from office. However, many don't resign. In the cases where they do, the odds are good that they will be replaced with a legislator who has an equally antigay record. After all, most of these politicians come from pretty conservative parts of the country. And the Republican Party doesn't seem too damaged by these scandals: The base just writes off the politicians as a few bad apples or accepts the narrative that being gay is an affliction requiring therapy."[1]

Some could also argue that it comes with the territory of being an avid homophobe. But despite the short-term gain (and joy) of outing a homophobic politician, it doesn't change how homophobic the Republican base is, and it does harm our ability to support and encourage a variety of romantic choices. It also contributes to the belief that being gay is an illegitimate act that people get caught at (and that needs to be cured).

And while politicians have always engaged in marital transgressions, there seems to be a newfound interest not just in holding them accountable, but in catching them in the act. This "gotcha" game is symptomatic of an audience obsessed with voyeurism (what else could explain the onslaught of reality television?), who yearn to learn the real dirt of a person's character to then judge them and use that dirt to determine their politics and their character. Politics has become a national soap opera, where we are more fascinated with our politicians' love lives and marital statuses than we are their actual positions.

Rather than infidelity being a rallying cry for why heteronormativity is not working, it instead exists as a way for politicians to one-up each other by focusing on questions of morality and shame.

The prevalence of these scandals hasn't opened up a conversation, as it probably should have by now, about our unwavering belief that heteronormative coupling is the only normal and appropriate way to structure your life. (I realize that would be asking a lot, but can we at least drop the "sanctity of marriage" bit?)

And though we seem to be particularly obsessed with playing "gotcha" with male politicians, it's important not to overlook the fact that female politicians and their romantic choices come under scrutiny, too. Sarah Palin's appeal to the religious right, after all, had to do with the way she played up what an average Nancy next-door stay-at-home mom she was (even though she was not). Palin's ability to capitalize on her puritanical identity was so strong that when she did have an accusation of cheating thrust at her, she managed to evade its damage.

Compare Palin to Hillary Clinton, who despite staying with her husband after his extramarital affair, is continually chastised by the media for being a "ballbuster" because she refuses to play up being a wife and mother and instead focuses on political issues. (This is not to deny that Palin also received sexist coverage, but it's important to note how each woman's romantic choices impact how the media chooses to portray their behavior.) In a similar vein, judges Sonia Sotomayor and nominee Elena Kagan were scrutinized for their single status, and later characterized by the media as lesbians. Why is it when women in the public eye don't live up to their ascribed gender roles that they are desexualized and painted as castrating figures that are a threat to our understanding of gender?

In 2010, when Al and Tipper Gore decided to call it quits, claiming it was mutual and cordial, the media became obsessed with what we didn't know, asking, "Was it terrible all along?" What they failed to take into account was the fact that theirs had been a successful marriage for forty years.[2] Sadly, while making mockery, playing guessing games, and being obsessive of people's romantic lives, we not only violate their privacy and air their dirty laundry, but we reaffirm the unrealistic expectation that the only lifestyle that's acceptable is a straight, monogamous, married one.

Feminists have long taken issue with the idea that heterosexuality, and therefore heterosexual pairing, should be mandatory. Betty Friedan's *Feminine Mystique* led the charge by highlighting married women's unhappiness in the 1960s. In 1980, Adrienne Rich's groundbreaking essay, "Compulsory Heterosexuality," argued that heterosexuality makes way for a "male right of physical, economical, and emotional access" to women. Today, queer scholars such as Michael Warner have challenged the idea that pushing for "normal" relationships results in pushing alternative lifestyles and sexualities to the sidelines. The political push for the "sanctity of marriage" is a hidden narrative based on fantasy, not reality. The overreliance on these stories to date, in the face of so much infidelity, only highlights the declining power of these illusions.

Motherhood, Family, and Nation

So now that we have a sense of how being straight and in a relationship factors into national politics, it's important to look at how gender and race play into what is considered "normal." One notable feature of Barack Obama's candidacy was the national fascination with his relationship with Michelle. And though I admit

I was taken with the fact that they were an attractive, young couple in politics that actually *looked* like they were in love, Michelle Obama's transformation in the wake of her husband's rise in popularity was striking. In a few short months, Michelle Obama went from being an extremely successful Harvard-educated lawyer, unapologetic about her often left-of-center viewpoints (and clearly someone as focused on her career as her husband, if not more), to a well-coiffed Mom-in-Chief whose pet issues included childhood obesity, gardening, nutrition, and supporting families of soldiers.

Despite the importance of these issues, she clearly chose areas of focus that played up her more traditionally "feminine" and "mother-like" qualities, removing her from hard-hitting (male-dominated) policy issues. Many feminists felt frustrated with this display of a more traditional type of femininity, and it is unclear if it was her choice, or a choice made on her behalf by the Obama PR team. Regardless, the media ate it right up (even now mostly focusing on her fashion choices—which in fairness are exemplary, but I digress) and she has definitely bought into the image. (Rebecca Traister talks about this in her book, *Big Girls Don't Cry*.[3])

But it's not really as easy as blaming Michelle Obama for not being as radical as we want her to be. Racist constructions of black motherhood play a large role in how she is perceived, and she has to work double time to avoid being cast as an "angry black woman." Michelle Obama had to win the appeal of the American mainstream with qualities that make her seem like she'd be a good First Lady: being feminine, appeasing, and focused on home; being successful in her own right (but willing to give it all up for her husband's career and her children's well-being) is just an added bonus. Her choice (even if on behalf of their PR team!) to play up her more traditional leanings has a lot to do with the fact that American conceptions of black motherhood not only are racist, but harmful in how they position black motherhood in opposition to white motherhood as a type of failure.

Don't believe me? Think about how differently Sarah Palin's campaign coverage would have looked had she been a black woman. Palin was a working mother with five children, one of whom, Bristol, was a teenager and pregnant while Mom was on the campaign trail. If Palin had been black (or Latina for that matter) she would have been cast as ignorant and uneducated and characterized as a drain on the system. Heteronormativity is not just about being straight; it is also about class, race, and lifestyle choices (Tim Wise talks about this in his essay, "This is Your Nation on White Privilege").[4]

Michelle Obama faced an uphill battle when she made a play for the national imagination as an acceptable candidate for mother not just to her family, but also to the country. First ladies must carry the legacy of femininity for the nation and embody what it means to be a woman, wife, and mother so seamlessly that we take it for granted. My own mother, whose role as a wife and mother fulfilled a cultural and nationalistic role and expectation, exemplified the role of a woman not just as a wife and mother, but the holder of culture (in our case, Bengali). Things I took for granted, like the fact that she cooked Indian food, or maintained Indian aesthetics in our home, were expected of her not just because the cooking and the maintenance of the house were a female roles, but also because they are traditional aspects of Indian culture. When I was young, I saw her insistence on keeping everything just so as a reluctance to change (and boy was I frustrated about it), but as I got older, I saw that it was about more than tradition, it was about nationalism.

In both U.S. and South Asian contexts, motherhood is represented as a constant and sacrificing role, where all other needs are put before the woman. This is so ingrained into the very definition of mother that it seems natural and normal, and sometimes it's even a point of pride. In post-occupied India, mothers were expected to hold the culture that they would pass down to the next generation. Transnational feminist Tanika Sarkar writes in her book, *Hindu Wife, Hindu Nation* that the new Hindu family was not just a family, but "the household is our motherland, that family is our India."[5] Mothers and wives were not just birthing and teaching their children, they were birthing and teaching a nation. And for those families who left India for the U.K., United States, and elsewhere, the stakes were that much higher: as a mother you were bringing your country with you to your new homeland, and you were wholly responsible for making sure your offspring fell in line with those same ideals. This deeply held political belief was inextricable from a cultural value and it was a core ideology my parents brought with them when they moved to the States.

Sarkar, along with other transnational feminists, such as Marnia Lazreg, Emma Pérez, and Minoo Moallem (among others), have pointed out that most countries, at their moment of inception or after a disruption such as war or revolution, overemphasize the family structure and the rightful place of women. These structures and roles reassure the people and uphold the values that the culture holds dear.

This was the case in the 1940s in the United States when women left the home to work during World War II. Shortly after the soldiers returned, however, there was a push to reconsolidate family values and many questions arose about the rightful role of women in society. Women were urged to take their position back in the home (and kitchen), while men went about rebuilding the economy and the nation. In the 1950s, the new American family was pushed through advertising and television with the birth of June Cleaver-esque images permeating popular culture. In *The Boundaries of Her Body*, Debran Rowland writes (in a chapter aptly titled "Turning from Rosie to June"):

> *"On October 4, 1957, the nation got a glimpse of the new American archetype of the woman-housewife-mother when* Leave It to Beaver *made its network debut. In a skirt that may or may not have sported a poodle, a top made of well-tailored lines, and a face aglow in makeup, June Cleaver baked cookies in high heels, offered sensible, lady-like advice to stymied children, and smiled lovingly over dinner with Ward. She was the 'perfect' fictional wife, mother, and woman."*[6]

Women were expected to stay home, yes, but it was dependent on class and race—something that's largely overlooked when we talk about that era of our history. Working-class women and women of color already worked before the war and were not in a financial position to return home to fulfill cultural and traditional expectations. But the family idealized as portrayed by the media and marketing of the 1950s was white and middle-class and had a stay-at-home mother who was in charge of all domestic tasks and a father who worked a regular job. Women's magazines of the day were full of advice to wives for how to take care of their husbands after they returned home from their jobs.[7]

A lot has changed since our parents' and grandparents' time, but the relationship between motherhood, family, and nation is still very much at the core of conservative legislation. The conservative fight to "take America back" is literally being waged on women's bodies with bill after bill trying to limit access to reproductive health technologies and make cuts to family planning. Melissa Harris-Perry of *The Nation,* in a piece about the right-wing war against women, wrote, "While leaving abortion nominally legal, cuts to family planning services and the legalization of terror against abortion providers would create an environment of compulsory childbearing."[8] Women who can't control their reproductive choices can't live freely and make choices for themselves about their lives and careers; they are forced into the domestic sphere. The continued push by the "moral majority" to clamp down on women's rights is reminiscent of the politics of the 1950s in its attempt to renegotiate the rightful place of women.

Today, despite the evident strides we've made (in some places) to be more progressive and inclusive about what we consider a family, and a complete shift in the economy requiring that women work, alternative family structures are still demonized. The "family values" ideal is so strong that when you go against the grain, either through same-sex relationships, interracial relationships, queer relationships, cohabitation, single parenting, or just being a single woman in your thirties (oooh, so avant-garde!), you are constantly defined and limited by the ethos of "family values" and the rightful place of men and women. On the one hand, we worship motherhood, but motherhood without a father in the picture is reviled.

The pressure to have a specific type of family and to be a certain type of woman impacts ethnic, racial, immigrant, and religious communities in unique ways. Even though I'm well into my thirties, I still have to deal with the social expectation that I should end up marrying someone South Asian American (well, at this point anyone will do). And despite the many options the young South Asian women I know had, when it came to dating, the majority of them married other South Asians. And I think there are a couple of reasons for this. One of them has to do with growing up in a country where you are the "other," which draws you to people whom you identify with and you feel can understand your experience. Another is a desire to preserve your community, culture, or religion (which is sometimes a conscious desire or sometimes just assumed). When you are an ethnic, racial, or religious minority, there is always a fear that your community is threatened by extinction. The result is often a reinvigorated sense of "family values" and what makes a good (insert ethnicity) wife. Today I have a better understanding of the nuances and choices immigrants have to make in the name of assimilation (but not at the cost of obliteration), but the limits of such a family structure cannot be ignored.

The pressure to marry is tied to what you represent in your community, but also to how you become an adult. Even in today's society, people are not considered "adult" until they marry. It's one of the markers that we've achieved what's expected of us and are on our way to starting a family. This means that if you are part of the queer community, you are perpetually a child— denied access to not only the social institutions that allow you to become an "adult," but also to all the cultural privileges and community support that come with getting married. People who live on the margins—whether we're talking about single women or queer couples—are accused of living irresponsible and/or immoral lives, and are often characterized as having made a "choice" not to grow up.

I never dreamed of growing up and getting married (it wasn't punk rock enough), and it turns out that my quite liberal parents have accepted me for who I am. What I wasn't able to articulate until I was older and found feminism was that it wasn't the "get married" part that bothered me, but the assumption that the only path for a young woman is to one day be a wife and mother. This politically motivated and culturally mandated necessity is a manipulation of our dreams and self-realization, especially as women living on the borderlands of gender, race, class, ethnicity, ability, and sexuality in the service of a romantic narrative that we didn't create for ourselves. If the assumption is that as a woman you have to one day be a (hot) wife and mother, any deviation is considered illegitimate, "alternative," or just a straight-up failure.

A Radical Imperative for Marriage

The hypocrisy of "family values" and the desire to keep women complicit in the traditional role of wife and mother has become apparent through the resistance to legalizing gay marriage. The insistence on keeping marriage between a "man and his wife" has become particularly vigorous as the religious right works to deny civil rights to the gay and lesbian community. The fight for same-sex marriage has shown us how homophobic and hateful some Americans actually are, and how tied they are to institutions that normalize binary and essential differences, such as marriage, the military, immigration policy, and healthcare (to name but a few).

The conflation of religious propaganda from the Far Right and the supposed moral majority with legislation denying same-sex marriage rights is evidence of the disdain for those who defy the "sanctity" of heterosexual marriage.

And how sacred is marriage? I am surely not the first author to cite in her book the statistics on how many straight marriages end in divorce, but they bear repeating. Fifty percent of first-time marriages end, and the numbers only increase for second and third marriages.[9] According to the Centers for Disease Control, in 2009, 2,077,000 people got married, making the national average approximately 6.8 per 1,000 people. Comparatively, 3.4 per 1,000 people got divorced.[10] What these numbers tell us is that what is heralded as a sacred and holy institution is not really that sacred. Marriage is not a permanent state, but a fickle and very much impermanent one. Marriage is a ritual, and many, many people go in and out of it as they please while others don't even have access to it.

Throughout history, marriage has been a right worth fighting for, a civil right. In eras past, marriage was an important part of survival and personhood. For example, during the antebellum era, there was a rich history of love and marriage that saw many slaves enduring tremendous circumstances to honor their marriages, using marriage as a way to carve out space for their personhood and spiritual strength in the face of an oppressive and abusive state.[11] It is not possible to compare the oppression mandated through enslavement to the way people are denied marriage equality today, but the point stands that marriage has been and can be used as a way for communities to maintain roots, garner protection from the state, maintain their spiritual awareness of and connection to each other, and build the support they need to live successfully.

It is hard to believe that until 1967, miscegenation (meaning marriage between a white person and a person of another race) was illegal. That was the year that the Supreme Court ruled in *Loving v. Virginia* that antimiscegenation laws were unconstitutional, ending all race-based limits on marriage. To this day, many intolerant people still find interracial marriage inappropriate and unnatural, including Keith Bardwell, a justice of the peace in Louisiana, who refuses marriage licenses to interracial couples. Interracial marriage was pre-1967, and in some places continues to be today, a political act.[12]

Meanwhile, any current radical imperative for love through marriage seems to have faded as the country fights over the issue of same-sex marriage. State-by-state bans on gay marriage have put the same-sex marriage debate front and center. With no thanks to a government that has been infected with religious propaganda and swung to the right, our romantic choices have become exceedingly scrutinized. The passage of DOMA in 1996, signed into law by President Bill Clinton, propagated the idea that the family as an entity had political significance, and that in the United States a family meant a married man and woman and whatever offspring they might bear. This legislation conflates marriage with personhood and citizenship, limiting marriage to certain groups and therefore giving those groups a privileged status.

In early 2011, the Obama administration issued a statement that they would no longer support DOMA because it "contains numerous expressions reflecting moral disapproval of gays and lesbians and their intimate and family relationships—precisely the kind of stereotype-based thinking and animus the (Constitution's) Equal Protection Clause is designed to guard against." Despite this pleasant turn of events, President Obama's position on gay marriage has always been neutral.[13]

The notion that civil unions are enough for gay and lesbian couples is not good enough. Many argue that marriage is what you make it, so what's the big deal if you can have similar rights in a civil union instead of a marriage? The problem lies in regressive policy that dictates the parameters of what a legitimate marriage is, so that even when you are a civil union you are still not considered "legitimate." Marriage is not just a personal choice, but also something recognized by the state that garners you specific protections. Because of this, the fight for same-sex marriage rights is important for symbolic reasons, and because these rights are civil rights.

While everything around us is changing, the definition of marriage seems to stay constant. The legal, moral, and political necessity of same-sex marriage is apparent, but the cultural and financial implications of the same-sex marriage movement have not been perfect. The mainstream gay rights movement has invested millions of dollars on the issue of same-sex marriage with an overemphasis on normalizing what "gay" means. (Lisa Duggan called this homonormativity.) The entire conversation around alternative sexualities—single-dom, quirkyalone, open relationships, polyamory, and other types of relationships—has been hijacked by the gay marriage conversation, having the effect of usurping the dialogue.

In 1999, sex activist and academic Michael Warner, in his book, *The Trouble with Normal: Sex, Politics, and the Ethics of*

Queer Life, wrote that he sees marriage as a type of "selective legitimacy." About marriage he wrote, "[S]tand outside it for a second and you see the implication; if you don't have it, you and your relations are less worthy. Without this corollary effect, marriage would not be able to endow anybody's life with significance. The ennobling and the demeaning go together. Marriage does one only by virtue of the other. Marriage, in short, discriminates."[14] Warner's radical interrogation of the reasons the queer community could not get married became the stand-in radical feminist/radical queer argument against gay marriage. Sexuality rights activists who were against gay marriage largely saw the fight for it as an attempt to normalize the queer community. According to them, extending marriage rights to same-sex couples didn't go far enough in changing the institution of marriage. In their eyes, marriage was still a site of unquestioned patriarchal, economic, and social control.

The last decade has shown that the fight for gay marriage has been an important agenda of the mainstream gay movement, whereas lesser-known queer organizations have been focused on different issues, such as teen suicide, runaway gay youth, issues of access, displacement, public safety, sexual assault—and the list goes on. Also, issues involving single motherhood fall squarely in the camp of the antiheteronormative and are rarely talked about as part of the marriage equality conversation. (That said, the most radical activist would tell you gay marriage should be legal, even if they differ on prioritizing the issue within the queer movement.)

There is only so much public space that can be devoted to alternative sexualities, and marriage equality has taken up a lot of the space (due to external and internal conditions). And while it has been a strategic choice on behalf of the mainstream gay rights movement, and telling of how homophobic this country still is, the conversation still hasn't hit upon the root of the problem, which is that to be considered a legitimate American, you should be married. The battle has been the fight for normalcy, but the product has been an attempted invisiblizing of alternative sexual identities or experiences, including both circumstantial (lovers kept apart because of immigration status, single mothers who don't get state support, incarcerated populations) and chosen (open relationships, polyamorous couples, nonmonogamists, singles, cohabiters). In a fight for normalcy, the mainstream dialogue around marriage is having the effect of creating buy-in from homosexual couples that marriage is, indeed, the more legitimate option.

Current mainstream conversations on love and marriage do not leave room for a radical imperative for love. The family values, gender identities, and choices that are upheld in popular culture as the right or best "choice" or way to live have implications for young people as they figure out their own identities. Mandatory heterosexuality impacts a multitude of communities. Young people internalize messages about what is the appropriate way to express their sexuality in a world that has shown clear hostility to any sexual transgression, or anything that falls outside of the gender binary. These retrograde, negative, homophobic, and sexist attitudes about love and life are what cause homophobic bullying. Our call to action is twofold: first we must fight for the rights of those who don't have full marriage rights to have those rights, and second, we must push against the limiting and exclusionary options that currently exist for how to live out our romantic dreams.

CINDERELLA 2.0

NEW ERA, SAME OLD FAIRYTALES

All too often, "falling in love" with the fantasy of romantic love becomes the aphrodisiac, rather than learning to love the real person and in real conditions of existence.

—Chrys Ingraham

{ CHAPTER THREE } Bridezillas, princess weddings, knights in shining armor, and the quest for the perfect body have saturated our brains. More than any other form of media, reality TV has filled the national imagination with toxic, exaggerated, and distorted visions of love, romance, femininity, and masculinity. If anything, the onslaught of reality TV shows dedicated to the embarrassing things people will do and say in the name of romance has shown us that there is a reinvigorated obsession with the romantic fairytale.

Turn on any episode of *The Bachelor*—the now famed reality TV show where twenty women live in a house together working to build a relationship with one guy who gets to choose whom he wants to marry at the end—and you will be confronted with a visceral stream of romantic desperation. Women with jobs, careers, and so much going for them are at the altar of our pity because they can't find love—and this is their chance to. The lessons these shows offer us actually serve as reminders of how much we still need feminism, truly. Lesson 1: All women are incomplete without love. Lesson 2: There is a shortage of men and so we must compete against other women to find love. Lesson 3: In order to find love you have to be beautiful and want the help of any and every product you can possibly imagine to enhance your beauty. And Lesson 4: There is no obstacle too large to overcome for true love, or rather, for that perfect wedding.

Today, reality TV is the great disseminator of romantic fallacy, hinging as it does on the most tired and played stereotypes about dating, romance, and gender. Jennifer Pozner writes in *Reality Bites Back: The Troubling Truth about Guilty Pleasure TV:*

> "... ABC struck gold with The Bachelor ... Why? Because this genre that calls itself 'unscripted' is carefully crafted to push all our culturally ingrained buttons. In the case of dating shows, it's precisely all the pretty-pretty-princess twaddle that allows us to accept these regressive notions as palatable, even ideal. Dating back to our earliest childhood instructions on gender, the call to these contrivances is powerful. The psychological underpinnings of fairytale imagery provoke a strong emotional response, and thus compel us to keep watching."[1]

And it is precisely because it is so hardcoded in us to see romance in this very particular way that they impact our psyches so deeply, even when we profess that we watch these shows for pleasure.

Obsession with romantic fairytales has opened up a large amount of cultural space for an industry with serious financial, social, psychological, and political implications. Romance today is not just about genuine ways to show your amorous feelings. It is a full-on "industrial complex" and it includes everything from the stories we internalize about romance to the actual romance-related goods we are urged to purchase to make us believe in that specific romantic experience—whether it is to look "hot" or to have that "perfect" wedding. The romantic industrial complex is a machine that involves many industries (including mainstream media, television, publishing, movies, jewelry, clothing, vacations, chocolates, alcohol, and more) working in tandem for your buy-in. And don't think for one minute that it doesn't impact how you think about romance.

An industrial complex is a series of organized institutions that inform each other and produce a specific outcome. Dwight Eisenhower first used the term to refer to the military. (The military industrial complex describes all the different components that make up that institution—everything from policy relationships between the government and the armed forces to the industries that support the production of military-related goods.) Activists and academics applied the phrase "industrial complex" to frame complicated interrelationships and so it's been adapted to describe other institutions as well, such as the prison industrial complex, the wedding industrial complex, and more recently, the nonprofit industrial complex.

Industrial complexes are symbolic for their interrelatedness, and that they create situations, mind-sets, and entire belief systems that are difficult to break out of. Suggesting something we all participate in—like romance—is an industrial complex shows us the ways in which we are all involved in networks of connectivity and how our experience of romance is impacted by forces we may or may not be aware of. The choices we make when it comes to love (where to travel, where to marry, where goods will be purchased, where goods are being produced) are laden not just with market value, but also with a high emotional value that manipulates the consumer into conflating purchasing something with attaining, affirming, legitimizing, and/or validating your love.

Fairytales about romance ruin our ability to connect with each other authentically. They put undue pressure on men and women to look and act a certain way. They determine the outcomes of our relationships, even when we don't think they do. When most people talk about the romantic industrial complex, they are talking about the wedding industrial complex, but it is not just when you get married that you all of a sudden feel the enormous pressure to love in a certain way. The rebirth of outdated fairytales in modern times impacts how we date, how we look, and if we marry.

Chivalry Is Not Dead, But It Should Be

As I was completing this book I started dating someone I really liked. A few weeks in, he lost his job and, much to my chagrin, disappeared. When we picked up communication later, I asked what had happened. He told me he didn't feel like he could date me without a job or any money. This seemingly antiquated reaction speaks to how deeply ingrained the message is that men should have to pay for dates, and that doing so is critical to dating and romance. This guy's sense of self was connected to his need to pay, and it was not something I could talk him out of; it had been burned into his psyche. But in trying to do the right thing and be the "good guy," he was inadvertently reinforcing sexist ideas of chivalry.

Chivalry, at its root, assumes male domination and female subservience. The term "romance" comes from the European Christian tradition, and it's most associated with the idea of chivalry and virginity. As Jessica Valenti writes in *The Purity Myth,* the notion of virginity "has always been deeply entrenched in patriarchy and male ownership." Similarly, chivalry and romance are very much tied to ideas of ownership and gendered expectations of behavior. Men paid for everything because women were considered property.[2]

Chivalry was romanticized through theater, poetry, literature, and music. Similar to today, love stories normalized gender difference in love, the belief that chastity was virtuous for women, and that men had to be knights in shining armor. Romance became the normal way through which intimacy was expressed. And whether we see Enlightenment-era European ideas of romance as silly or not, they continue to influence current stories about romance. Modern-day fairytales of imagined romantic lives assist us in turning a blind eye to the actual costs associated with romance—physical, emotional, and financial.

Today, traditionalists decry the "end of chivalry" and how popular ideas of feminism ruined romance. We have already covered the problems with this characterization, but suggesting that feminism ruined romance is appalling. This essentially claims that despite all the progress we have made where women are concerned (access to resources, education, labor, and capital), we've done ourselves a disservice because women no longer being reliant on men and male power (a.k.a., male money) is somehow unattractive. Civil rights, it would seem, are unromantic. Men and women who believe in chivalry are seen as the modern-day keepers of romance. They're the ones who espouse that, yes, all that equality is cute, but at the end of the day don't all women want a knight in shining armor?

And when it comes to dating, money equals power. Money and romance are interrelated both in how we accept and how we reject where the power lies in a relationship. Men are expected to pay. Men who can't foot the bill are cheapskates, scrubs, and losers. Women are expected to want a man with money, but if she vocalizes this need she's a "gold digger." Women are expected to spend money to look a certain way to meet a man. And if he does pay, she puts out. Money guarantees an all-access pass to the vagina park.

The opposite of the "he buys, she puts out" romantic story is the one where women have all the power. This gets played out through expectations: She has money, so she should split the bill, cover her half, and shouldn't "expect it all"—meaning she shouldn't expect to have her freedom *and* expect a man to pay for everything. When women pay for their half of the date or their own wedding it's considered feminist. When a woman makes out with a big divorce settlement, it's considered empowerment. If a woman makes too much money, it's emasculating. The competing stories are mind-numbing. What it should come down to is who can afford what, but that would be too much common sense for something as irrational as romance.

You might be wondering—*so what's wrong with someone doing nice stuff for you?* Romance without the pressure of money and consumerism is *beautiful*. There are few things as satisfying as dating someone you really like: going out to a delicious dinner with them, having someone make nice plans for you, walking home together, and that kiss—that kiss! People who are dating *should* take care of one another and do nice things for each other. And then there's all those little moments you get to celebrate once you've been with someone for a while: being together, the whirlwind of nostalgia, sentimentality, and memories that are created to reflect back on. And while it's clear that many of those moments are influenced by external factors, we still *feel* them, and they feel *good*. Romance can truly be a celebration of the potential for human capacity, connection, love, sex, and our hope for the future.

Similarly, in parts of the queer community, romance is alive and thriving. When a butch or stud acts out stereotypical types of chivalry, it doesn't carry the same cultural weight as a cis-man ("cis" means someone whose gender performance matches up to their biological sex) carrying out the same actions. There is a difference in power between how straight people realize romance versus non-heteronormative couples who often don't benefit from cis-privilege or even the ability to express their love legally, safely, or with freedom. Perhaps this gives more space for experimentation without the baggage of sexism (perhaps it doesn't, that's another debate), but it does shed light on the performative nature of gender, and challenges our assumptions that romance is natural. We perform romance, we fetishize it, and we play with gender within it.

The performance of chivalry isn't inherently bad; it is the gendered expectations that are. Gender is a fundamental part of how romance gets played out. Who is expected to do what, who calls whom, who makes the first move—all of these are gendered and put pressure on both parties to act a certain way. I have heard both men and women complain about the gender-related pressures associated with romance and dating. Men don't want to always have to make the first move and women don't always want to feel like they have to wait or be passive. Romance, as we're spoon-fed to believe it *should* look, is a big spectacle.

And it's not just about symbolic gestures, like holding the door open. If you identify as a feminist and tell a guy you're dating that you are, then you've likely been on one of those dates where the guy says, "Well, I won't hold the door open for you then," or, "So I guess that means you want to split the bill?" This focus on simple gestures obscures the real needs feminists have when it comes to how we date. It is not about holding the door open, and it's not about the bill; it's about recognizing the ways in which gender is connected to power and how those power imbalances play out when we're dating. The notion that getting the tab or the door means getting the vagina is hardly what we think of when we think of romance, and yet we're socialized to believe that this is in fact what romance is building up to.

Chivalry is outdated; it exploits perceived differences between men and women. And often, people like it that way. They get high off the power imbalance because it's sexy, feels traditional, and is associated with our understanding of destiny and what we *should* be doing. Today, even though the way men and women interact has changed, romance is still based on the idea that interactions between them are a fetishization of unequal power relations between genders. And this is not only harmful to women; men don't benefit from these renderings, either. It puts them in a position of being either the good guys, who know the rightful duty of a man is to pay and take care of you, or they're bums and cheapskates. The expectations of people based on gender as part of our typical romance stories are problematic and don't help any of us further our quest in finding authentic romantic connections.

Fat Girls Don't Get Dates

So forget the chivalrous knight in shining armor—what about that hot, demure princess? Fairytales tell us men not only should have all the money, they should have the physical power as well. Prince Charming should be able to carry you, so if he can't, well . . . it's because fat girls don't find Prince Charmings. The pretty-pretty-princess complex is not a particularly new one, but it's particularly salient with the rise of shows like *America's Next Top Model* (part of the Tyra Banks empire—a tragic but addictive show about women trying to become supermodels), *Make Me a Supermodel* (wherein Tyson Beckford and Niki Taylor teach you how to walk, talk, and dress like a supermodel), *The Biggest Loser* (where people compete to see how much weight they can lose), or *I Used to Be Fat* (MTV's bid for our obsession with weight loss that features young people who commit to losing weight between high school and college so they can start a new chapter in their lives).

The romance industry conflates finding love with looking a certain way, and it's hard even for the strongest of us not to internalize messages about the way we look. And worse, these messages are normalized. Just think of things people say when they are getting ready to date someone: "He's cute," "He's short," "He's kind of chubby," "He's tall and fine." Or men, "I prefer slender girls," "I'm not really into fat girls," "I prefer Asian chicks," and on and on. It is completely acceptable to say the most appalling things about the way people look when it comes to dating, and if someone is called out for it, their opinion becomes a matter of "preference."

What gets ignored in calling this level of categorization "just preference" is a history and culture of mainstream advertising that impacts our psychology, causing us to actually want to respond to certain things over others. It's hardly a coincidence that people are attracted to images of femininity that have been beaten into their psyches. In Chapter 1, I talk about Cordelia Fine's idea of associative memory and what happens when we see certain images with repetition. We are taught to prefer certain things over others, and when we repeatedly see the same exaggerated images of femininity and masculinity, we internalize a specific standard of beauty and begin to strive for it unconsciously. Considering the exaggerated nature of these kinds of images, preference is not really a "preference"; it is more like a culturally sanctioned fetish.

Attraction is not just about a feeling. It's a heavily mediated experience and part of an industry that pumps billions into creating images of what women should look like. It can be hard to decipher what you are attracted to versus what you have internalized as attractive. This goes for both how we see ourselves and how we see others, and it leaves a lot of room to fester for some really messed up ideology about size, race, and sexuality. White standards of beauty get conflated with romantic ideals and create Cinderella-esque ideas of what romantic femininity should look like, all serving to uphold a certain standard of beauty. This impacts our self-esteem, the kind of energy we put out there, the types of people that are drawn to us, and ultimately who we end up dating.

Mainstream media is saturated with exaggerated caricatures of femininity, from Beyoncé to Joan Rivers. If you were to put together a manual today based on popular conceptions of what it means to look like a woman, using the cues of our day, you would find that women should be young, light-skinned, wrinkle-free, hairless "down there," big boobed, curvy (but not too curvy), thin, and ultra-super-feminine. Thanks to these impossible-to-reach media conditions, women deeply internalize the belief that if you don't look a certain way, you are not going to meet a man. The beauty and body industry grosses millions every year by feeding off the insecurities of women, reiterating this already internalized belief that who you are—the way you are—isn't good enough. You best get to spending tons of money on everything from mascara to boob jobs to make yourself attractive for your knight in shining armor.

The expectation that women be thin is already catastrophic. Eating disorders, body dysmorphia, and other obsessive habits about the body are at a record high. And while being obsessed with what you eat and how you look has somehow become so normal that we don't even flinch when our friends pick at their food, or spend hours in front of the mirror getting ready to go out, or try not to "look fat," the connection between these obsessions and the expectations put upon us by the romance industry is underexplored. Body dysmorphia and its associated manifestations run deeper than women's desire to find a date, but negative marketing that exploits this in the service of helping women attract men is downright criminal.

This pressure has removed us from being in touch with our bodies and disconnected us from being able to feel fully comfortable about ourselves when we're with the people we are dating. If the expectation is that we have to look a certain way to get asked out, if you don't, you start to believe you don't deserve to get asked out. We eliminate ourselves from situations, we are characterized as tragedies, and the world around us tells us how much better we could be if we could just lose those pounds and uncover the love life we have been missing out on.

Thankfully for fat activists, feminists, and the fact that people have different tastes, the negative associations with fat are being worked on. Women who self-identify as fat are finding love for themselves and on their own terms. Obviously, women who identify as fat go on dates, dress to impress, and find happiness in both their romantic and personal lives, but none of this is anything the mainstream media is interested in showcasing. Why bother? The new trend in reality TV is to depict overweight people losing weight, complete with sad stories about how they hate themselves, live the most depressing lives, and have never been able to find love. It's clear that popular culture has an obsession with ridiculing fat people, and Americans eat it up (pardon the pun).

A perfect example of the "fat girl as romantic tragedy" meme is Fox's reality TV show *More to Love*, which aired in 2009 and focused on larger women finding love. Beyond the fact that many of the women on the show weren't that "big," they spotlighted women's background stories as sad and pathetic and made sure to play up how they were denied love and intimacy because of their size. And it was emotional to watch; it played on people's deepest insecurities about not being attractive enough to find love. Although it touted itself as a show that would dispel the myth that fat women can't find love, *More to Love* only ended up reinforcing fat stereotypes, framing each shot with food and filling space with personal testimonials of young women who'd never found love because of how fat they were. Because what else are fat girls doing but sitting around and crying about their love lives while eating food? I mean, really?

I'm a fat girl and I have worked to maintain the belief that I am beautiful despite what the culture tells me about my weight. I wear what I think is cute, and yes, like most women, I sometimes obsess about my weight. But, I don't let being fat stop me from engaging in romantic relationships. Fashion, style, and being feminine have always been fun for me, not something I use to cover up who I am and how I look. But that doesn't mean it's been easy. Every time someone has not been interested in me, I've wondered if it's because of how I look. Like so many women, I carry the negative associations of what society thinks of as fat on my shoulders, and it has impacted how I see myself. It's a constant effort to reassemble your self-esteem every time you're rejected, and for many women it comes back to beating ourselves up for what we look like. It's a full-time job to reject the messaging that gets heaped upon us about whether or not we look attractive.

Buying into popular constructions of femininity is not always empowering. Popular ideas of feminism have mischaracterized the "beauty as empowerment" myth to include any choice any woman makes as okay, as long as she chooses it. But as long as the pressure to be thin and look a certain way fits into a larger story about princess fairytales and the subsequent money you need to spend to look that way, it is hardly an emancipatory moment.

Then there are the mainstream feminists who decry the way young women use fashion to express themselves, but here I actually see an opportunity for reappropriation in the face of a culture saturated with lookism. There is a marked difference between feeling pressure to dress and look a certain way for male attention (i.e. wearing miniskirts in the snow—bad move!) and using fashion as a form of resistance against a world that tells you that you're not worthy of love because of the way you look. If you allow it to be, your style can become an opportunity to engage in gender play. Fashion can be a fun way to express yourself, and can even be an opportunity to make a statement about things that really matter. Fashion can be feminist and an opportunity to fight back against dominant ideas of what we should look like.

From my perspective, young women have learned to manipulate and navigate, as they see fit, their self-expression through fashion while trying to make conscientious decisions about their love lives. This may sometimes involve playing into normative beauty standards, but young women also have to figure out what's come to be an increasingly difficult climate, where it's all about being hot or not, or fat or not.

Want to Get Married for Love? Think Again.

What is the point of acting the part and looking the part when it comes to romance? For it to end one perfect day with that big spectacular wedding, that's what. Love has been commodified and its ultimate expression is on your wedding day. Weddings encapsulate and hold up the values of the romantic industrial complex.

Feminists have talked extensively about the role of marriage in society—work that has been invaluable. But marriage today is no longer what it used to be. While social pressure to marry has changed ever so slightly, as have gender roles within marriages, the expectation and pressure to marry have shifted. Now it's coming from corporate interests, a trend that has two side effects: first, it locates the marriage industry within the global flow of goods and products, and second, it upholds one particular type of marriage over all others—the one that involves a princess fairytale wedding.

Weddings have become an entire industry unto themselves, and while the average American can't afford a big expensive wedding, advertisers are relentless in pushing their wedding-related products. Chrys Ingraham writes in her groundbreaking book, *White Weddings: Romancing Heterosexuality in Popular Culture*, that the "wedding industrial complex" is a "structure [that] reflects the close association among weddings, the transnational wedding industry, labor, global economics, marriage, the state, finance, religion, media, the World Wide Web, and popular culture."[3] When a couple decides to get married, they don't have to contend with just the social pressure to get married, but also the financial burden of the wedding itself as propagated through books and magazines, bridal showers, flower arrangers, caterers, and all the other players that make out because of wedding-day romantic fantasies.

Marriage defines the terms of our relationships more than

we'd like to believe. Unless you explicitly let it be known otherwise, the default position for all romantic situations is that they will end in marriage. In my opinion, the idea that it's all leading up to something—a series of celebrations and presents and hopefully babies shortly thereafter—is one of the most frustrating realities of dating. Not just because of the pressure it puts on your current dating situation or romantic relationship, but because of the pressure you feel when you are single and you *should* be out there looking for The One. And ingrained in all of us are the moments set up to lead to that one fine day when you'll marry The One you love.

Currently, there are a record number of couples cohabitating, and certainly you don't need to get married to have a child. Traditional marriage is dead, and upon examination of those high divorce rates cited in the last chapter, it's pretty clear that marriage is about as sound an investment as putting money into a used car that keeps breaking down on you. But despite all this, people not only crave the nostalgia a wedding offers, but financial, social, and cultural pressures to get married continue to be strong.

The economics of marriage are not to be taken lightly. Seventy-two billion dollars per year are spent on weddings, and over two million couples get married every year. According to the Condé Nast Bridal Group, as of 2006, the average wedding costs $27,852, and this statistic becomes even more staggering when compared to the reality that 68 percent of Americans made an average income of $25,000 in 2006. And this doesn't even take into account the cost of the pre-wedding festivities and the money all the guests have to shovel out on presents, getting to the wedding, and all other related expenses. Today, the wedding industry is estimated to be $161 billion.

I have had several friends who got married in the last few years and tried to go a cheaper route, and yet they were constantly harassed and haggled by wedding vendors (even a lesbian couple who was perplexed that they were expected to spend so much money for something that isn't even legally recognized!). Even when you want to do it for yourself, outside of the marriage industrial complex, it's practically impossible. And as any of you who have had to throw down for your friends' weddings know, the financial costs of a wedding that you're only attending as a guest can really rack up—especially if you have to travel.

And speaking of travel, Ingraham notes in *White Weddings* that wedding products being produced overseas are often coming from places that have unfair labor practices and exploitative working conditions. For example, in the 1990s, thirty-six female inmates in South Carolina were paid just pennies to sew lingerie for Victoria's Secret, one of many examples where a corporation "hired" inmates for labor.[4] In 2011, there was a campaign led against 1-800-flowers because they were buying most of their flowers overseas from flower plantations where workers were being exploited.[5] And we've all heard about blood diamonds.[6] All of these decisions have global, political, and economic ramifications most brides and grooms don't think about. The costs of wedding-related luxury commodities place you within a global circulation of products, goods, and money that have implications that are far from romantic.

I know, you're thinking—*but what else can we do?* After all, living in the United States assumes, on some level, living off the exploited labor conditions of others, so *what's the big deal about my wedding?* And many people do go to great lengths to find out who's producing the goods they purchase for their weddings; some of my friends hired locally, or hired friends to take photos, make the food, and arrange the flowers. Like anything you can buy into, the impact you have depends on your income bracket. Clearly your global impact is going to be different if you are poor and putting all your money into a humble wedding versus being filthy rich and spending millions.

People who are cognizant of the wedding industrial complex and all of its fallouts have lots of explanations for how their weddings were different. It's true; there is no way to be part of the Western industrialized world without participating in the machine to some degree. But that doesn't change the larger powers at play behind the scenes. It's not about individual weddings; it's about the entire industry and the impact it has on the global economy, on culture, and which supports how society gives preferential treatment to married couples.

Weddings aside, marriage garners you certain privileges, and as long as we're talking about straight marriage, it puts you into a desirable social, political, and financial bracket as well. It's a way to legitimize yourself in the world, and it makes you an adult. As someone who primarily dates men, if I were to end up in a situation where I needed to get married for financial reasons, I could; for me it *is* a choice. For many, it is not a choice, and I don't want to downplay the very urgent and necessary financial reasons for why equal marriage rights should be granted to all communities.

Marriage is fundamental to the way that society and capital are organized, and as a result it is connected to a slew of benefits. In *What Is Marriage For?*, E. J. Graff gives a compelling breakdown of why the gay and lesbian community needs to fight for the right to marry—and one of the main reasons has to do with the basic protection of financial assets and accountability of resources. She writes, "Say you're a stay-at-home mom whose husband doesn't hand over any money to buy groceries or pay the utility bills. Can you take funds from a bank account that's just in his name? Can you take him to court and insist he pay up? Can you get a court order blocking him from taking all the money to Vegas?" And while the answers to these questions vary by state, she makes a strong point that marriage law is society's way of deciding what's fair between married folks—and that's a protection that's not afforded to same-sex couples.[7]

But the many reasons why we have to fight for same-sex marriage rights doesn't change that politically and financially marriage is a huge piece of the economy and therefore comes with its own baggage. Financial protection is not something that is afforded to single people, cohabiters, single parents, or polyamorous couples. Exclusionary marriage laws and global consequences aside, marriage and weddings are very complicated decisions. And there are plenty of people—straight and not—who want to opt out completely.

But even for those who want to opt out, fairytale weddings still impact them, because they produce a nostalgia that has become synonymous with the right to marry.

Laura Kipnis writes about the strange obsession with rituals moderating love in her book, *Against Love*, saying, "A more accurate description of the situation might be that we've mortgaged our emotional well-being to intimacy institutions that hinge on elaborate fictions themselves, at least to the extent that feelings are unpredictable, that desires aren't always coherent or static, that knowing what you want in the realm of love and intimacy isn't an exact science, and people do occasionally change." Marriage being predicated on love and lasting forever is a fairytale that mainstream advertising, popular culture, and media support. This has made rational decision-making around the question of marriage practically impossible.[8]

As a result, young people, and especially young women, are limited, socially, culturally, and politically, where romantic relationships are concerned. Every woman knows that choosing to remain single, or to just live with her partner, or to have a child "out of wedlock" has some sort of financial and social consequence. She will either be seen as a courageous example of the successes of feminism, or as an example of the failures of feminism. If you don't get married in the name of feminism, you are a martyr for the cause. If you want to get married but feel guilty about it, you are a victim of feminism's antiromance, antilove stance. Feminism and marriage are constructed as two opposing forces, suggesting that they can't coexist.

The romance industry is not just about pushing people to get married and have really romantic dates—it's also about keeping women hanging onto the idea of fulfilling unrealistic fairytales. Women are bombarded with strategically crafted images and messages about how we should look and what we should be doing to catch the man of our dreams, but most of them contradict each other. Young women are expected to focus on dating, meeting a man, marrying that man, and living happily ever after, while being educated, having their own money, and becoming successful in their career. And whether you find happiness in your career, with friends and community, with hobbies, or with children, none of that is meaningful if you are going it alone.

Keeping women focused on finding the right man is an underhanded way to keep us acquiescing to traditional values. Conflating our self-esteem with our relationship status is a very powerful and effective way to keep women feeling bad about themselves. I mean, if being alone means you are essentially a social pariah, an outcast, a *feminist*, and potentially ugly and unlovable, you are not going to be seeing young women lining up for the role.

Freedom, liberty, upward mobility—all of these are values that women are taught they should be striving for from the time they're little girls—and yet they have all come to represent exactly what men should not want in a woman they're interested in, because somehow women who've attained all this cannot make good wives. Anne Kingston writes in *The Meaning of Wife*, "The characteristics associated with the traditional good wife—servitude, subordination, self-sacrifice, summarized in the pejorative *doormat*—were discordant with the qualities of independence, 'self realization,' and ambition glorified by the culture. Successful single women scoffed at the wifely role." Keeping women in two opposing categories—marrying material and not marrying material—doesn't allow for a middle ground. Wife assumes the past—servitude, weakness—whereas independent assumes assertiveness—money, power, career, and education. Both frames are predicated on privilege, however, since many women have to juggle both in varying degrees, and neither frame actually reflects how women live.[9]

The generation that is currently coming of marrying age—those women in their twenties and thirties—are faced with the wins and struggles of the women who came before us, meaning we have to navigate for the first time newfound freedoms juxtaposed against still-prevalent but antiquated ideas of our place and role in the world. It's a lot to have on our shoulders, so our attempts to make sense of it all and still find romance are a daunting prospect at best. We are told we can "have it all," and yet, if we are expected to fit into dominant fairytales about romance, we actually can't.

Despite the transnational social, political, religious, and economic implications of weddings, the idea of marriage is a beautiful (albeit unrealistic) one. And marriage is changing. Gender roles are morphing and access to marriage is slowly changing as well. But instead of pushing for a world where women can get married guilt-free, I think, as women, we need to push ourselves and really think about why we want to get married, what it still symbolizes, and how much of what we want is based on what we want versus what the fairytale ideal has taught us to want.

TOP FIVE SEXIST MYTHS

PUSHED IN POPULAR
books on dating

Obviously maintaining a relationship nowadays is something no one should attempt to do on their own—it's far too complicated for ordinary non-trained humans, like deciding to build your own telecommunications satellite and launching it into space.

—Laura Kipnis, *Against Love*

{ CHAPTER FOUR } As I confessed in the introduction to this book, I find myself drawn to the self-help section of the bookstore whenever I go through a breakup. This is when I feel the most motivated to take charge of my life, swearing I will never make the same mistakes again. I'm craving stories from other people about love gone wrong and all the ways in which they are *just fine*. Even in the best of circumstances, ending a romantic relationship has its challenges, including a fair share of sadness, fear, confusion, sometimes relief, sometimes bitterness, and the general feeling that you tried again and it didn't work out—*again*.

But the most popular self-help dating books these days don't often deliver what they claim they're going to, and almost nine times out of ten they actually make you feel worse. They profess to have the answer to your dating woes, but that answer seems to imply that you've done something wrong, or that there's something you could have done better. Being self-aware is great, but in the name of self-help, authors, gurus, and relationship experts alike often play the blame game, making women feel bad about themselves. And the messages are so insidious that we don't generally get the full impact of the message until it's too late.

Not every self-help book is bad, of course. Some are about healing, overcoming fear or shame, or supporting people to become their best selves. Those books are great. But, I'm talking about the popular dating books that are out there, including *He's Just Not That Into You; Don't Be That Girl; Why Men Love Bitches; The Case for Settling; It's Called a Breakup Because It's Broken;* and others that fall into the pop culture relationship advice category.

If you are like me, you may have read a few of the aforementioned titles and had a few aha moments, but overall it's likely that something didn't sit right with you. That's because they're riddled with problematic messages and they fail to recognize how sexism plays out in how we date and how romantic expectations play into our dating situations. Conversely, they almost always put the blame, responsibility, and success of relationships squarely on the shoulders of women, while writing off or justifying the behavior of men. They assume women are more invested in the success of their relationships, by nature, so they must do the hard work of making their relationships work. Ultimately, they rely on making us feel bad.

There is an entire industry committed to convincing young people to throw away their money in the name of romance, and the self-help industry is just one spoke in its wheel. Through magazines, books, and talk shows, the self-help and dating advice industry supports two things: the toxic fantasy of romance that we covered in the last chapter and the inherent differences between men and women. The self-help industry bills itself as being necessary for keeping young women on course to the relationship of their dreams, and thus we see related industries cashing in—through advertisements, marketing campaigns, self-help books—as they effectively convince women that being "in love" is what they need to find happiness.

Feeding the Fantasy

Despite its original intentions (which I have to presume were, in fact, about helping people), dating advice has by and large become dating propaganda.

The vast industry of relationship advice is profoundly effective in the psychological, creative, and intellectual manipulation of people's deepest insecurities about being alone. Through fetishizing the inequality embedded in the romance story, women have somehow been convinced that being in, or even vying for, a relationship is something we *should* want—regardless of whether that relationship might hold unequal power or doesn't serve us. Even when the relationship is detrimental to our independence, sense of community and friendship, and often our sense of self, being in a relationship is still more valued than not being in relationship. Just think how many friends you have lost to their relationships—and that it's considered an acceptable, even normal, absence. Our culture has grown increasingly couple-centric, so much so that when we're not in relationship we feel that something must be wrong, and we best get to fixing it.

If you lined up every dating book you could find in the bookstore, you would find that most advice is contradictory. One may empathize that it's normal that you feel desperate for love, but whatever you do, you don't want to look desperate. You want to look pretty (and waiting). Don't care too much about what you look like, but men don't want to see you in sneakers (always have lipstick and pumps at your disposal). You don't want to be too much of a bitch, but you don't want to be a pushover either. You should be independent, but not too independent (men, after all, like to feel in charge!). Don't act like you will cook every dinner, but you better know how to cook. Don't act like a slut, but it's good to be a whore in the bedroom. I hope you've been taking notes—it's hard to keep it all straight.

And who's that dude you're looking for anyway? These books are supposed to help you find the love of your life, but it can't just be any man. It has to be the right man: the man who is into you, who isn't an asshole, who likes to have sex like a "man," who has a job like a "man," who has friends like a "man." These books tell you that if a guy doesn't call you right away then he's just not that into you. They insist that most men are self-obsessed assholes (so really, why would you want to date them anyway?) and that if you want to find one of them and make them your husband you better bow down to patriarchy and get with the working order of things. They assume men don't change, but tell women they have to.

Conversely, men's dating books suggest that men should maintain their "cool" demeanor and make women feel so insecure that they will beg to be with you. They also support myths about how men can't and shouldn't seem to care too much, and definitely shouldn't call too often. Women are told not to call because men should make the first move and men are told not to call because if they do they will lose control of the situation. How exactly are young people communicating then? Well, that's part of the problem. They are not, really.

The lack of gender fluidity inherent in most dating advice is confining at best, and the list of contradictory messages is horrifying if you are actually looking for concrete advice on dating. It is no wonder that young women are confused about how to find actual love when they are trying to navigate a world that propagates so many different messages about how we should think, talk, behave, and interact.

The marked difference between dating books that are marketed to women versus the ones that are marketed to men is strategic. It is assumed that women vie for love while men just want to get laid. Steve Harvey, comedian turned relationship expert (three times divorced and accused of potentially emotionally abusing his last wife), and author of *Act Like a Lady, Think Like a Man*, said in an interview on *Salon* that he would never bother writing dating books for men because he would never make any money. It's women, after all, who have the burden of fixing their relationships. Women are the ones who are relationship-obsessed and high-maintenance, while men just have to deal with what a drag it is to keep women happy so they can dip the stick. Neither characterization is very generous.[1]

And I suppose it should be no surprise that the best-selling dating books are written by men, and that the most popular self-help gurus are men. There's Greg Behrendt, author of *He's Just Not That Into You*; Dr. Phil; Steve Harvey; John Gray, author of *Men Are from Mars, Women Are from Venus*; Travis Stork, author of *Don't Be That Girl*; and Jimi Izrael, author of *The Denzel Principle*—all bona fide dudes that hold the key to your love life, men who claim to understand women and naturally want to save them (how sweet!) from the pain they have inflicted on themselves (of course) because they tried to make sense of the actions of men. But silly girls! It's not the men who are wrong, it's you for believing they would or could or even should be any different than what's expected of them. That's right, if you want to find love, get high on patriarchy because that's the only way to do it. And beware, because many of these male authors posture as feminists, claiming that they are doing it for you, to help you and your emancipation.

There is a long history of men determining what is right for the mental health of women, starting with Freud and bringing us to current with Dr. Phil. The male perspective on love (and everything else) is generally the most respected. In writing her seminal book, *All About Love*, bell hooks found most well-known meditations on love have been written by men. She writes:

> "A woman who talks of love is still suspect. Perhaps this is because all that enlightened women may have to say about love will stand as a direct threat and challenge to the visions men have offered us. I enjoy what male writers have to say about love   Men often write about love through fantasy,

*through what they imagine is possible rather than what
they concretely know. . . . But, like many women and men, I
want to know about the meaning of love beyond the realm
of fantasy—beyond what we imagine can happen. I want to
know love's truths as we live them."*[2]

hooks is talking about literature and poetry, but her point about fantasy is useful. Male fantasy—what men want from women—is embedded at the core of how we understand romantic relationships. Whether it's conscious or subconscious, keeping women subordinate in a heteronormative relationship is a patriarchal-based fantasy. Patriarchy benefits from women staying in the dark, staying subordinate, and remaining clueless about what they truly want out of their love lives.

It's irrelevant whether these self-help doctors' intention is to emancipate women if there is no analysis of patriarchy and capitalism in books that claim to talk about love in contemporary society. And I can tell you based on my reading that the effort is coming up short. Failing to delve into these larger societal issues means sidestepping the root problem of why we are having a hard time finding love successfully. And there are a lot of men who feel trapped by the normative gender roles that are portrayed in these books, so the harm done is quite universal, not to mention that it completely ignores queer relationships and trans identities altogether.

And that's not to say that women dating advice "experts" don't fetishize the subordination/domination fantasy of the patriarchy. The most popular dating books written by women are the ones where the author has given up on trying to find love on her own terms, or has declared that feminism has ruined her sex life. In many of these books, the female authors suggest that if women want to be in successful relationships they better check their own success, independence, and ego. Thumb through a copy of *Why Men Love Bitches, The Case for Settling,* and *The Man Whisperer* and you'll see that they spit a similar narrative; they are all written by women who are all for independence and "girl power," but in reality they profess that success has ruined romance for them. In a world where sexism is still so rampant and where women are still judged by their marital status, and where so many young women still use male attention as a measure of their self-esteem, to suggest that women check their independence and ambition at the door is downright irresponsible.

If there is one thing people are insecure about it's their romantic lives, so you can see how dating books and advice generally are a tremendous opportunity for exploitation and profit. One thing you can count on our bloated, marketing- and product-obsessed culture for is making a lot of money on something you feel badly about. And what better way to manipulate the insecurities of women who are already bombarded with messages about why they can't find love? Marketing books to women for their most vulnerable time—post-breakup—is a surefire way to continually sell these stories. They play to our greatest insecurities, and as a result most mainstream dating books are ruining our love lives.

Sexist Dating Mythologies

As I mention above, the torturous yet telling experience of reading many of these books brought one glaring reality to my attention: There's no room for gender fluidity of any sort. When it comes to dating advice books, you are a "man" or a "woman," and how you react to things hinges on these designated and innate natures. There is no gay in dating, there is no trans in dating, there is no queer in dating, and there is no lesbian in dating—there is just man and woman.

Now of course there do exist some dating books and re-sources specifically geared toward these communities, but even this fact further validates my point: The assumption that straight assumes specific and rigid gender definitions disallows a produc-tive evolution in how we understand and act out our dating lives. Most dating advice only makes sense if it plays off the lowest common denominator of gender identification. And our reading of men and women is very simple. Women are complicated, shallow, insecure, materialistic, marriage-obsessed, and meek, and men are sex-obsessed, self-centered, selfish, unemotional, simple, and unchangeable. No wonder love is in a state of crisis. Have we not evolved at all?

Sexist Dating Myth #1:
You are not hardwired to have sex like a man.

You've undoubtedly heard it before: women can't (and shouldn't) have sex like "men." There is a lot of competing evidence that sug-gests men and women experience sex differently (more on this in Chapter 7), but it is hard to make a general statement about such a specific experience. Women are routinely shamed for having sex, while men are told they should be chasing tail, so it is almost impossible to generalize about who enjoys what.

One of the biggest myths about dating is that how soon you choose to have sex impacts the longevity of the relationship. So if you are a woman and you're looking for love, giving it up too early will preclude any possibility of a long-term relationship. Outside of being blatantly slut-shamey, this advice is plain wrong. In 2010, a study from the University of Iowa found that if two people wanted to be in a relationship, when they had sex didn't matter.[3]

When sex happens varies from couple to couple, and you can probably find plenty of examples of successful relationships where couples had sex on the first date, and plenty where they waited for months. Studies that claim it's waiting that makes a relationship last should at least address how those couples who do and don't last communicate around sex and their relationship, since my guess is that good communication, regardless of when a couple chooses to have sex, plays a huge role in longevity.

Not one of the books I mention in this chapter asks whether men themselves feel it's important to have sex like "men," or whether men even like having sex like "men." After all, does having sex like a man make you a "man," or someone deliriously detached from your emotions and therefore unable to participate in one of life's greatest physical pleasures? The idea that men are pussy-chasing unwieldy man beasts who can't think straight since their main goal in life is sex is highly problematic. *Most* guys aren't like that, and most guys you want to date are offended by this characterization of masculinity.

The result of these kinds of characterizations, however, is silence around how men experience sex, since there is so much pressure for them not to have feelings about it. Ultimately, it's the advice men get about how to be in relationship that hurts the longevity of relationships, not women who are open to having or want to have sex on the first or second date.

Suggesting women shouldn't have sex too early as it ruins their chances for true love is slut-shaming with new packaging. Instead of stuffy white religious dudes telling you not to have sex and putting out retrograde policy to exert control over women's sexuality, you instead have seemingly nice guys who "get it," or women who have survived the dating trenches and are telling you the real deal. But it's really two sides of the same coin. These authors may not blatantly suggest that you are a slut, but through nuanced advice like, "Don't give it up too early" and "Never have sex on the first date," you start to realize that women are expected to give the illusion of chastity if they are looking for love. In *Be Honest—You're Not That Into Him Either,* Ian Kerner even went so far as to blame second-wave feminists' sexual empowerment for ruining our ability to have good relationships. Kerner writes:

> *Men are more than content to accept a world where there is sexual equality and where women can take charge— we just don't know how to handle it quite yet. The potential downside to a scenario where women are as aggressive as men, and where casual sex is an accepted norm, is that it essentially gives men license to be, well, men. The biggest beneficiary of this female empowerment is the male. That is not to say that women should play by certain "rules" or withhold sex. That does not work, and it's silly gamesmanship. Or is it?*[4]

It's clear that Kerner himself gets trapped in his own truth-telling because the premise of his book makes no sense if men still can't handle it when women are in control. In this view of the world, you have to figure out what you like and go get it. He tells women that they can't have sex like a man, but they should feel empowered to have sex like a man. But if they're too aggressive and have sex like a man, they might be contributing to the problem, which is letting men get away with having casual sex. Doing this results in ruining women's chances at landing a good man, and yet if they don't do all these things then they will end up alone.

The Kernel of Truth

It's true—there are guys who just want to have casual sex, just like there are some women that want to only have casual sex. But those aren't the people to be chasing down and trying to have relationships with. And as the old adage goes, it can only get better. Where sex is concerned, this is generally true. You meet more confident partners, more people who are comfortable communicating their needs around sex and relationships. In the meantime, if you are not looking for a casual relationship, it's good to know what you want, whether casual or more serious, and eliminate partners as you see fit.

Sex is emotional and communication only makes it better. Sometimes waiting allows two people to get to know each other in a way that an immediate hookup may not allow. If that is what you feel like you need, do that. Waiting to have sex can also be really hot, and although it probably won't affect the longevity of your relationship, it might make the sex better as you get more comfortable with someone and are able to tell them what you want from them.

But "holding out" for the sake of holding out only feeds into sexist stereotypes about what men and women want from sex. Don't focus too much on the sex part of it; it is the communication that makes it better, and this is something that can happen whether you have sex early or not.

Sexist Dating Myth #2:

Women should NEVER ask a guy out.

In 2004, motivated by a scene in *Sex and the City*, one of the writers of the show, Greg Behrendt, wrote a book called *He's Just Not That Into You*. It was wildly successful, especially after Oprah touted the book as the answer to saving women's love lives.

The book is simple: If a guy doesn't call you back, if he doesn't ask you out, if he falls off the planet, he is just not that into you and he's an asshole. Sounds harsh, right? Well, not to the author who claimed to be helping us confused women get the skinny on men in his no-nonsense guide to dating. This book was conceived to help women understand what they are doing wrong in trying to figure out these misunderstood man-boys.

The general framing of this book is deeply problematic. It is predicated on the belief that the reason women shouldn't worry about men who don't call them is because women shouldn't ask men out. Men like to be the aggressors. Behrendt writes:

> Men, for the most part, like to pursue women. We like not knowing if we can catch you. We feel rewarded when we do. Especially when the chase is a long one. We know there was a sexual revolution (we loved it). We know women are capable of running governments, heading multinational corporations, and raising loving children—sometimes all at the same time. That, however, doesn't make men different.[5]

Without even realizing it, Behrendt ruins his own thesis. Women can be empowered, even sexually empowered, but basically men aren't going to accept that so you might as well wake up to that fact and get with the submit-to-patriarchy program. It's clear that in his world, if you want to date, if you want this relationship of your dreams, you have to accept your subordination. Reading between the lines, the conclusion is that we live in a world where "empowerment" is something men joke about because it gave them access to "more pussy, man!"

Full disclosure, I tried Behrendt's advice and guess what happened? Time and time again, guys thought I was not interested in them because I never called them. I waited for them to ask me out, but they were too intimidated, so I didn't get asked out. Unsurprisingly, not all men are assholes; some of them are actually scared because we are so amazing and together and clear about what we want in this world. To them it's obvious that if a strong, independent woman is interested in them, she will let them know.

And what do guys think? Well, I did a random survey (yes, very scientific, I know) of my male-identified friends and asked them if they feel uncomfortable or think it's bad when a woman asks them out. Every single one of them said no—that it is either flattering, relieving, and that often it makes them like a woman more. A few of them said it makes them uncomfortable if they don't like the woman back, but hey, doesn't that make all of us uncomfortable? I do realize that according to the *HJNTIY* paradigm, these guys I asked may not qualify as "real" men; however, the reason *HJNTIY* isn't working as a means to getting the romantic relationship of your dreams is because gender norms have changed and it's now okay to ask a guy out. It is archaic (and a little weird!) to sit back and wait for someone to call (text, email, whatever) you. Does that mean there are guys who prefer to ask girls out? Yeah, of course there are, but in my experience, if someone likes you and wants to go out with you, who asks who out has very little to do with how the relationship is going to turn out.

The Kernel of Truth

Despite my objections to the overall premise of *HJNTIY*, the idea that we might need help understanding men in and of itself is not particularly offensive. It's good to recognize when you are dealing with someone who is emotionally immature and giving you the runaround, and sometimes we need to be reminded to just let it go, move on, and not give someone any more chances because they have shown you nothing but bullshit. *HJNTIY* can be relief for women who are constantly agonizing over problematic behavior from men, or making excuses when someone is really giving them the runaround. It is not that they are not that into you; it's that they don't have the respect or skills to effectively convey what they want from you.

Also, it can be difficult to call a man when we're being convinced left and right that doing so makes us desperate and needy. You don't want someone to think you *need* them. And as independent women, we face a dilemma: We recognize that men have a lot of power, we want to defy that power, and yet we still want to date without getting cast into the sexist trope of being the "needy chick" or the "ballbuster." Why do we look needy when we call someone, when in reality we are just busy and in all likelihood more plan-oriented? I have accomplished every other dream in my life and then—bam—when it comes to dating, you are telling me I have to wait? Oh, hell no.

So while it may be true that there are some men who feel

uncomfortable when women ask them out, most guys are into it. So take a risk and defy what's expected of you. And if you get rejected, remember it doesn't diminish who you are or your potential to meet someone else. At least you were courageous enough to try and that is what empowerment is all about.

Sexist Dating Myth #3:

Men are simple, women are complex.

The mere fact that so many of the self-help books out on the market are geared toward helping women figure ourselves out reinforces the idea that we are way too complex, and that we need to get a grip on our manic, obsessive, and unstable selves. We think too much, talk too much, and ask too many questions. Behrendt states that men are simple, yet they are running the world. If they want you they will go after you. How a man is complex enough to run the world, but too simple to be able to date complex women, I will never understand.

Jimi Izrael writes in *The Denzel Principle*, "Men are not complicated creatures and don't ask for much. All we want is a woman to work, cook, clean, and maybe give up a lil' booty on our birthday." When people say "men are not complex," what they are saying is that men are comfortable with the status quo, because they benefit from it. Don't mess it up with your women's lib and all those needs you have. That's when things get complicated.[6]

Don't Be That Girl is the book in which Stork lists all the types of girls you might be but definitely don't want to be. We are so complex we need an entire book to dissect all the different ways we might show up in relationship. He includes Lost Girl, Working

Girl, Desperate Girl, Insecure Girl, Bitter Girl, Yes Girl, Agenda Girl, and Drama Queen Girl. The book is really more of a read into the complexities of male hatred for women. If I were to write a book about male stereotypes, I would call this author Misogynist Guy.

Most of these labels are self-explanatory, but a few really stick out for their blatant sexism. For example, let's look at Working Girl, the girl who is so obsessed with her career she has no time for men:

> The type of Working Girl I am referring to is not the highly functioning career woman who has managed to strike a healthy balance between her professional and her personal life. No, the woman I'm talking about is the one who hides behind her career. . . . But you can tell that she's using her job as an excuse—whether she means to or not—to avoid getting involved with a guy when she says one of her catchphrases:
>
> "Men are intimidated by my success."
> "I have no time for dating."
> "My work fulfills me completely."[7]

So basically you are damned if you do, damned if you don't. Don't be too career-obsessed, but don't be too needy, lest you become Needy Girl. And Working Girl's catchphrases are actually pretty accurate. A lot of men feel bad about themselves next to successful women (remember, the media is telling men they are not "men" anymore), a lot of women don't have time for dating, and many women are fulfilled by their work. These ideas about women are sexist, and you can recognize them as such because when men say the same things it's not considered weird or different.

The only difference is that people get confused when a woman doesn't spend all her time vying for a man.

Both Stork and Behrendt (not Izrael, he's a mess) recognize that patriarchy still exists, and yet they conclude that women should accommodate this reality. In fact, part of the problem, according to them, is that men have a hard time handling how far women have come. They also both recognize that you need to have your own thing going on, but not enough to distract you from your primary goal, a.k.a., that dude! They are both so unapologetic in their self-consumed man-centric view of the world, it's no wonder they don't see their own contradictions. And I can pretty much guarantee that if you asked either of these authors why they continually focus on what women should do instead of what men should do, they would reply as astutely as Steve Harvey did: Men aren't interested in this kind of advice.

Men are never held to the expectation that they should have to balance their careers with their personal lives; it is considered totally acceptable for them to give everything to their careers. There are men who are engaged in their personal lives, of course, but there is no social pressure or expectation to be this way. None of the That Girl categories make sense when applied to the normative male gender. They only make sense if you believe that women are girls and subservient to men in relationships. They also only make sense if you believe women/girls are objects to be studied, categorized, and understood for their "complexities."

Stork's hypothesis illuminates the heart of the contradiction. Men are capable of doing all the same things women can do, except when women do it, it is considered complicated. The self-help industry capitalizes on characterizing women as needy, wishy-washy, demanding too much, and being unstable, which makes us think we are more troubled and complex than we are. Perhaps male simplicity comes from the internalized recognition that patriarchy benefits them, so they never have to change or feel bad for having their own needs met; it's only women who have to feel bad. Why do women have to apologize for being able to do it all? Why do I have to worry about offending someone with how complicated I am? Shouldn't men be the ones reading self-help about how to deal in a world that is not as reliant on unequal gender relationships? Shouldn't they be the ones getting up to speed?

The Kernel of Truth

Let's face the facts—everyone is complex. We live in a transnational, global, local, and online world. We all participate in multiple identities at once, and if that doesn't make us complex, I don't know what does. So while women may be constructed as complex, men are complex, too.

Also, women from way back have always been challenged with the necessity to multitask; we have had to hunt, gather, till land, raise babies, educate those babies, all while getting dressed and making sure everyone in our families has everything they need. Women are complicated because we are expected to do it all, but then when we do it all successfully we are told we won't get laid or have a boyfriend. Real generous, guys.

Sexist Dating Myth #4:

It's only okay to be a certain kind of bitch.

The term "bitch" has become synonymous with modern feminism

in many ways (partially thanks to *Bitch* magazine) because young feminists have reclaimed the word. For some of us, being a bitch is something we take pride in because it means we won't take shit. We don't smile just because you ask us to, and we get what we want without waiting around for it. Obviously, in the world of heteronormative dating, this type of bitch is a major boner-killer, unless it is done to an acceptable degree. And what is an acceptable degree of bitchitude (as blogger AngryBlackBitch puts it)? Sherry Argov, author of the best-selling book, *Why Men Love Bitches,* explains:

> Certainly, I'm not recommending that women have an abrasive disposition. The bitch I'm talking about is not the "bitch on wheels" or the mean-spirited character that Joan Collins played on Dynasty. Nor is it the classic "office bitch" who is hated by everyone at work.
> The woman I'm describing is kind yet strong. She has a strength that is ever so subtle. She doesn't give up her life, and she won't chase a man. She won't let a man think he has a 100 percent "hold" on her. And she'll stand up for herself when he steps over the line.[8]

At first glance, it almost seems like we should strive to be a bitch, except that Argov doesn't diminish sexist uses of the word "bitch" in her book. No, she fully acknowledges that there are those kinds of bitches, but you should work to be a different kind of bitch. You should be the kind of bitch who doesn't make men feel inferior.

It would appear serious bitches still pose a threat to the patriarchy. Argov is trying to redefine "bitch," not for the purpose of fighting for a world where women aren't perceived as bitches for getting what they want, but to manicure ourselves into the kind of bitches men like.

When a woman is a bitch in a situation of assumed hetero-normativity, she is frequently isolated, or put in her place by a man. I say this not only from personal experience, but from witnessing friends who have shown they are aggressive, or not pushovers; and then when they go after what they want, someone tries to put them in their place. Perhaps Argov doesn't realize that she's saying only certain types of bitches can get a guy. When men like bitches, they want the type of bitch that is attainable and ultimately can be controlled. We feminists know that a real bitch does not get down like that. A real bitch is someone who understands power relationships enough to know when to be nice and when to be a bitch. And a real bitch is not going to be nice just to get a guy, unless he is a guy who is not threatened by the fine art of bitchitude (to borrow Shark-fu's phrasing).

The Kernel of Truth

Prevailing attitude is such that when a man feels threatened or emasculated by a woman who's a "bitch," they either ignore, insult, or try to control that woman. This obviously doesn't hold true for every man, but if you encounter a guy who displays any of these attitudes toward you, walk away and save your bitchitude for a more worthy fellow.

I asked one of my girlfriends—someone who would definitely identify as a bitch—what her experience with men has been. She told me what I already knew. When we are nice, people think they can take advantage of us and often ignore or overlook our needs. But when we make clear what our needs and wants are (allegedly bitchy behavior), they get met. I don't think the author of *Why Men Love Bitches* would necessarily disagree with that assessment, but the key difference is recognizing that the pejorative form of bitch is something inscribed with sexism and that the only way you can change your bitchitude to please men is in your servitude. I don't know about you, but I am way too big of a bitch to allow that to happen.

Sexist Dating Myth #5:
You have to be a bad girl in the bedroom
and a good girl in the kitchen.

That's right, you have to be two people at the same time. I already touched on the prevailing idea that women are not capable of having sex like "men," but there is another age-old standard around sex that women are expected to live up to: the very sexist but timeless virgin/whore dichotomy. This refers to the idea that there are some women you have for sex and some women you make your wife, and their qualities shouldn't coexist in the same person. Both connotations—of women as whores or virgins—are based in sexist understandings of women and sexuality. The first shames women for being sexually adventurous, suggesting they are so low they are like sex workers (in effect shaming, silencing, and invisiblizing the lives and experiences of sex workers). The second assumes that women are only good when they are pure, as in virgins. The confusing part is that we are often expected to be both, and while these are the two extremes and no one actually lives up to either (effectively), these categories inform how women are judged.

How many of you have been called bad girls for being sexually liberated? It is a common experience, and it is an effective way of pitting women against each other. "Whores" are bad girls you have to protect your men from, while wives are good girls that men can take home to Mom. Argov, even while demanding that men love bitches, admits that men like a ho in the bedroom and a mama in the kitchen and "[w]hat a nice girl should know is that even if you make every effort to be an exemplary housekeeper, he'll still want a ho behind closed doors." It's all very confusing, isn't it? And at what point do we concern ourselves with what makes women turned on, excited, and happy when it comes to sex?

The Kernel of Truth

Sexist beliefs around what women's appropriate sexuality is have made it difficult for women to break free from the virgin/whore dichotomy. We cannot have the relationships we want to have if we feed into this concept, and we must push the men we date to confront their stereotyping. The more women resist being treated and/or labeled this way, the more men will take notice. Interestingly, the ho in the bedroom idea has become quite popular lately with women taking pole dancing classes in the suburbs and stories of sexual experimentation within the confines of heteronormative marriages, showing how experimentation and reaching outside your comfort zone can bring excitement to tired marriages.

But this doesn't take away from the fact that the mainstream conversation around what's appropriate and acceptable is still framed with this idea that there are good and bad ways to be sexual. When you have deeply embedded stereotypes, oftentimes women unconsciously choose one over the other, disallowing a more nuanced sexuality that is much more complicated than "good" or "bad."

When Did It All Get So Complicated?

So, you make it through the proverbial wilderness of dating and you find someone to date consistently. All of a sudden you are living a dream, the dream you are supposed to live, but you aren't happy. You notice that you are acting in ways that make you unhappy. You are "giving in" and losing independence. You start talking about how unhappy you are, and you feel like you need something different. So maybe you try an open relationship because you don't want to lose the guy. Or maybe you try things that are totally outside your comfort zone—threesomes, some kinky stuff—but ultimately you are not getting to the root of what is not working for you and there is no book that can explain it. All of a sudden you've checked the "it's complicated" box on Facebook and you realize it *is* complicated: you have sex with other people complicated; you don't spend time together complicated; you don't actually have sex with each other complicated.

But is it really relationships that have gotten complicated or has the world just changed? And what is the opposite of the "it's complicated" paradigm? Doesn't everyone wish to be able to love as they please, gender irrelevant, marital status irrelevant, even immigrant status irrelevant? No, being normal and uncomplicated means shutting up and doing what you need to: settle down with a nice, well-behaved, handsome-enough man who has a good-enough job, get married, have a big white wedding (actually, you should also probably *be* white, or middle-class, or some such variety of the "normal" subset), make some normal-enough babies, and have your normal and uncomplicated life. You might even go so far as to support gay marriage, as long as they don't replace yours. Simplicity is actually a lot more complex than we realize, but it is when you diverge from this path of simplicity that things really get "complicated."

The really complicated part that no one seems to be talking about is that the gender differences purported in mainstream dating advice books lay the groundwork for intimate partner violence. As daters, we are bringing with us our histories and often those histories are filled with pain and either physical, sexual, or emotional violence. Researchers have estimated that 17 percent of all women and 3 percent of all men are survivors of some form of sexual abuse; it bears examination, and should be addressed in any book about intimacy and relationships.[9] Too many survivors are never able to discuss their experiences with their partners, and the advice I've read doesn't create space to be able to do so. If anything, these books and authors support a society that allows for intimate partner violence to be the norm by setting up the power inequalities that allow for it to flourish. What we need is advice and space to help us heal from the wounds of living in a world with such rigid definitions of gender and unreal expectations from men and women.

Naturally, when you have an entire segment of the population functioning under the belief that they are not only too complicated, but have also failed at finding love effectively, you can get them to buy products that purport to make them feel better. The demand, therefore, for material about love, romance, dating, and marriage is telling of the pressures women feel to find "love"—and I specifically put that in quotes because it is not just about finding love. We love our friends, our families, and even our lovers, but what so much dating advice assumes is that women need to find love within the confines of marriage, with a husband. That is what's really meant by love. And according to this paradigm, the only time we should love ourselves is when it will help us meet a man.

These prevailing attitudes about dating will only lose steam if we start by rejecting this type of advice and telling our friends we don't want to hear it. We need to blog about it, yell about why it is unjust and wrong, and let people know that it doesn't accurately ring true to our lives, realities, dreams, and goals. We need to push back. We need to focus on communication between young people and not shame women for having sex or shame men for having feelings. As much as I am tempted to say fuck you every time a guy does wrong by me, it feels better to know *why* it happened. Without an analysis of power, mainstream dating advice only hurts us. Only once we reach a point where we can recognize that men get hurt from acting "manly," and women are hurt from men being "manly," can we stop the cycle of feeding into regressive and restrictive gender expectations in our love lives.

SINGLE
AND LOVIN' IT!

Sorta.

Settling soul mates? That's grim. And I've played Monopoly alone!
—Liz Lemon

{ CHAPTER FIVE } Single gals are the talk of the town. Beyoncé's track "Single Ladies" was the 2009 anthem for single gals who have said enough is enough with the runaround. If you like me then you should "put a ring" on "it"—or I am moving on. "Single Ladies" is hardly a feminist anthem. It equates committed relationships to marriage, asserts that marriage assumes ownership, and feeds into the idea that you need to be either "single and lovin' it" or "married."

But hey, it's popular culture, so if we ignore what's problematic about the lyrics momentarily, we can thank Beyoncé for giving voice to the idea that single ladies have options and men be warned: If you don't make a move, you will lose your lady. It's true, not all single ladies (or gay men—let's be real, we know who loves this song the most) want to get married, but we can all relate to dumping someone who didn't want to commit to be single only to later find out the person you dumped is jealous of your newfound freedom. And although the song concludes with a desire for the dumped to become Prince Charming and come around (again, it's popular culture), the point stands: Choosing single life over an unfulfilling relationship is not an easy choice to make. And in my opinion, this is all the more reason to celebrate it.

The very notion of the "single woman" is fodder for fantastical storytelling. The single woman is one of the most reviled yet beloved mythical characters. She is always painted with superhuman characteristics and piled with expectations she would never be able to live up to in real life. At her most idealized, she is a superwoman, doing it all on her own, balancing her career, sex life, education, employment, friendship, and sometimes even motherhood, all while looking super hot and being unbelievably happy. But when she is not the stereotypical bubblegum popular culture notion of the "single gal about town," she is at her most reviled and feared: on welfare, representative of the failure of femininity, a threat to masculinity, a threat to the family, a spinster, a cat lady, bitter, alone, jealous, never been kissed, and I could go on. The portrayal of the "single lady" is ripe with contradiction, both in terms of how much people overemphasize how empowering it is to be single and how much our culture uses single women as examples of failed femininity and spinsterhood.

Single women interrupt the ethos of heteronormativity with a frustrating persistence because, as a whole, single women are succeeding at a faster rate than many other groups. Outside of simply creating a lot of ego hurt for modern conceptions of masculinity, the side effect of the supposed rise of the single woman is woman hate, backlash, and overstated declarations that women "have it all." Whether we're talking about stories about divorcées who are sucking their ex-husbands dry (how can we forget Alec Baldwin's "man"ifesto that gave new language to the real victims of alimony payments—men), black welfare moms who are feeding off an overburdened system (*16 and Pregnant* did not help our cause here), or single mothers with too many children (think "Octomom"), the images in the media of single women (and especially single moms) are appalling. And if we're searching for powerful or successful examples of single women, the images are not much more forgiving: think Elena Kagan, Sonia Sotomayor, Martha Stewart, and Oprah (who is in a long-term relationship but never married), all of whom are considered castrating and desexualized, and/or to be lesbians, in addition to being powerful. Femininity and power, it would seem, are mutually exclusive.

Single women's stories are often stories of success, of choice, of failure, of overconsumption, of overburdening the system, *and* of being social pariahs. The identity of single women is always wrapped up in their marital, romantic, or parental status. Single women are anything we want them to be, but whatever they are, we are obsessed with their lives because they disrupt mainstream notions of gender, relationships, and family.

Lore has it that women are fine being single and making choices for themselves, but structurally there is very little support for single women, especially single mothers. And women who do it on their own bear the financial, social, and emotional cost of being single in a society unwilling to truly support their lives. We are painted as sexy, sinful, successful, and pathetic—you name it, both good and bad—but ultimately we live outside the norm and are not ultimately considered a success.

Where Have All the Strong Single Ladies Gone?

From *The Mary Tyler Moore Show* to *The Bachelorette*, there has been a marked shift in how single women are portrayed on television. Sitcoms of the '70s, '80s, and even the '90s portrayed single women as complex, working, humorous, powerful, and oftentimes happy. Today, sitcoms do not hold the same cultural importance they did in previous decades, but reality television does and has filled that void, pushing images of single women as depressed, "catty," and desperate for love. Along with this shift in how single women are characterized on television, there has also been a change in how single women (and all women on television) look, the more recent images reflecting corporate-fed images of unattainable "beauty."

Television is a reflection of our cultural norms at a given time, so it makes sense that during the '60s and '70s—a time of cultural revolution where the very definitions of family, sexuality, relationships, and femininity were being pushed—women were written as living comfortable, fun lives as single women who engaged in sex when they wanted it and often opted out of long-term relationships. *Laverne & Shirley,* at the height of its viewership, was the most watched sitcom in the United States, surpassing

Happy Days, which is shocking considering its often serious and feminist themes. *Laverne & Shirley* took on unplanned pregnancy, sex before marriage, and workplace equality.

In the 1970s, '80s, and into the '90s, lead single ladies continued to be written as strong, assertive, and independent, as seen in shows like *The Mary Tyler Moore Show, Good Times, Kate & Allie, Murphy Brown, Living Single, 227,* and *The Golden Girls,* all of which showed women as complex and strong and subsequently garnered tremendous viewership. Each of these shows had strong single (whether divorced, unmarried, or just unexplained) female characters that hailed from a variety of social classes, ethnic backgrounds, geographical locations, and age ranges.[1]

If we look to the sitcoms of today, we see weaker depictions of women dominating the tubes. We see women who are smaller in stature, more neurotic, confused, wishy-washy, and often dysfunctional. There are few sitcoms about single women even on the airwaves today, actually. But think of the leading ladies in sitcoms, from *Everybody Loves Raymond* to *The King of Queens;* both Debra and Carrie represent good, faithful (and hot) wives. And while the plotline shows they are often the ones in charge, their story lines are secondary to their goofy, irresponsible, "bro-ish" husbands. While these characters' behavior could be chalked up to the shows being satirical or humorous, there is a noticeable difference between how women and their romantic relationships have been represented over the decades.

Similarly, if we are to look at the representation of single black women even from the '90s to the new millennium, a quick comparison of *227* and *Living Single* to *Girlfriends* shows you how differently actresses are cast today. Earlier shows cast black women of varying sizes, skin tones, and hairstyles, whereas more recent shows seem to only cast thinner black women with straighter hair and more Caucasian features. Let's just acknowledge that you don't turn on the TV and see a great actress like Esther Rolle these days (unless you're watching *The Biggest Loser*).

Sitcoms have become less culturally influential than they were thirty years ago. So while shows like *30 Rock* intentionally jab at some of the stereotypes of how single women are represented (Tina Fey is our feminist hero), it's hard not to connect the rise of consumer images of women that cater to antiquated ideas of femininity and post-'80s feminist backlash with the way women are represented on television today. If current manifestations of women in the media tell us anything, it's that our cultural comfort level with strong, independent women has shifted from interest and acceptance to mockery.

To characterize this mockery we need only look to shows such as *The Bachelorette, I Love New York, More to Love,* and any other show that is about single women looking for love. Or better yet, as I mention in Chapter 3, check out any episode of *The Bachelor* and watch beautiful, successful, single women fall apart in front of our eyes as they get eliminated from the show (and kiss their chance of marrying Prince Charming goodbye) and cast off into spinsterville. Sitcoms about single women in the past carved out cultural space for a feminist identity based on independence and complexity. Reality television gives us nothing but images of women who are broken, pathetic, and simple in their base desire for romantic fulfillment.

Popular television has changed, but what has entered the public domain are new caricatures of femininity that play to our most regressive stereotypes of how single women should think, talk, and act. And while reality TV is supposed to be "real," the images of single women have only gotten less real. According to reality TV, all single women want to get married and their lives are meaningless without this milestone, despite any personal or professional successes they might have seen. This has closed up any real possibilities for characterizations of single women as anything but failing at the dream of romance.

The Feminist, Fantastical World of *Sex and the City*

Reality television is the primary reason sitcoms have become less popular; another is the rise of cable television. Networks such as HBO and Showtime portray much more nuanced female characters, single and otherwise. This is evidenced by shows such as *Weeds* (Mary-Louise Parker's character is not your average single mom, to say the least), *Mad Men* (artfully showcasing the sexism of the '60s), *Six Feet Under* (who didn't love Brenda and Claire?), and *The Wire* (Kima and Snoop are both very complex characters).

Where regular network television is concerned, the now off-air *Sex and the City* takes the prize for its nuanced characterizations of single women. I know, up until now you were hoping I wouldn't dedicate a whole section to the over-referenced holy grail spectacle of single women in the city, *Sex and the City*, but I must do my obligatory analysis of the show that in many ways defined popular culture perceptions of single women in the '90s and new millennium. And I'll disclose a little secret: I was a huge fan of the show. Women everywhere loved *Sex and the City*, and a big reason why was because it showed us a new type of single girl.

Sex and the City (*SATC*) ran from 1998 to 2004 and painted the picture of four women who were supposed to represent different types of femininity. We had Charlotte's obsession with traditional romance and family, Samantha's sex addiction/relationship allergy, Miranda's ball-busting "classic feminist" pragmatism, and Carrie's shoe-obsessed, boy-crazy, self-absorbed, writer, fantasy lifestyle (really, introduce me to the person who has an amazing apartment in Manhattan who writes one column per week). And depending on the season and the episode, all four women vacillated between being single, in relationships (casual and serious), married, or divorced.

There was supposed to be something for everyone to relate to in *SATC* and women ate the images right up—myself included. *SATC* was a fantasy, a portrayal of a grown-up life that seemed like the perfect example of modern life for women integrating gross materialism with a sense of independence while still having it all. Full of witty repartee, *SATC* became a popular culture stand-in for mainstream and modern feminist ideas about sex and romance. Finally, we thought, a show where women were talking about relationships and sex in frank and honest ways, along with showcasing noncompetitive female relationships similar to those of the sitcoms of earlier decades.

It was clear from its inception that *SATC* was intending to rewrite the modern female romance narrative, pushing it outside the realm of finding Prince Charming and happily ever after. The foundation of the show was simple: material gains for women equals independence. And although it was a mainstream feminist narrative, the characters' habitual materialism was anything but feminist. Despite this, in the beginning, *SATC* engaged in very feminist themes, showcasing casual sexual relationships, female friendship, and a lot of dialogue around the oppressive structure of heteronormative coupledom. *SATC* was explicit in showcasing four women who embodied different forms of "choice" feminism. Each of them had clearly chosen the life they wanted to live, the men (and in some cases women) they wanted to be with, the jobs they wanted to have, and the shoes they wanted to wear.

There were several episodes that directly attempt to disrupt ideas of heteronormativity and marriage. In "A Woman's Right to Shoes" (Season 6), Carrie is at a party where she is asked to take off her $485 Manolo Blahnik shoes because the party hosts have children. At the end of the party, Carrie discovers that her shoes have gone missing, leading to a series of uncomfortable interactions between Carrie's friend Kyra, the hostess, and Carrie. In one scene, as Carrie attempts to get her friend to acknowledge that her shoes have gone missing, Kyra's response is that she can't be asked to pay for Carrie's extravagant lifestyle since she has a "real life" now. Carrie responds that she has a "real life," too, but the scene ends awkwardly. The exchange prompts Carrie to realize that she has spent over $2,300 on Kyra, between weddings, wedding showers, baby showers, and birthdays, which forces her to reflect on the ways we're expected to throw money at couples.

In a scene that follows between Carrie and Charlotte, Carrie airs some of her frustration, saying, "And if I don't ever get married or have a baby? What? I get bubkes?" She decides that she will marry herself and registers at Manolo Blahnik. She leaves Kyra a message saying, "I wanted to let you know that I'm getting married. To myself. I'm registered at Manolo Blahnik. So thanks." This forces Kyra to buy Carrie her shoes and also makes the point that the choices we make as single women are choices we have the right to make. And they can be equally indulgent as the choices those with "real lives" make. The episode concludes with Carrie's voice narrating, "The fact is, sometimes it's hard to walk in a single woman's shoes. That's why we need really special ones now and then. To make the walk a little more fun." Gross materialism aside, this particular episode did an excellent job of airing a lot of the anxieties placed upon single women about their choices, their lifestyles, and how they spend their money.

Another episode from early in Season 2, "Four Women and a Funeral," touched on this theme as well. Miranda is trying to buy an apartment in Manhattan and realtors keep asking, "So it's just you?" "And the down payment's coming from your father?" and she is forced to repeat, "Yep, it's just me." After surviving the repeated humiliation of filling out multiple applications that require her to check the "single" box under her status, she starts to have panic attacks because she is afraid she will die alone. It's ludicrous, it's hilarious, and it is television, but the sentiment is a real one. In real life, women are often questioned about their single status, what has caused this appalling condition, and what are they doing to change their status, as though being single is an anomaly or a downright tragedy. And how do single women make all those big decisions like buying houses and cars without a man in their life?

Both of these episodes spoke to the quiet narrative in our culture that tells us if you are a single woman and haven't settled down with a man and/or started a family, you don't fully under-stand what responsibility means. This is not to downplay the tre-mendous responsibility that comes with raising a child, or to judge the choices of people who are coupled, but the problem lies in the assumption that single women are vacillating, unsettled, and self-indulgent while coupled parenting life is hard and requires sac-rifice. This characterization of single women doesn't allow space for them to be seen as independent beings, but instead as always being in a middle space waiting to be put in their rightful place as a wife and a mother.

After the series ended, the two *SATC* movies left us with a legacy of cultural insensitivity and male obsession. Everyone ends up in a committed relationship except Samantha, who is left, ste-reotypically, fighting old age with all types of newfangled ways to beat menopause (and at one point is characterized as overweight). The writers apparently finally capitulated to popular fears of rela-tionship failure and felt the need to draw the characters as settling down with boyfriends that soon became husbands.

Most problematic at the conclusion of the *SATC* film was Car-rie's decision to settle down with six-season lurker, Big, despite the fact that she was defined as being the woman who questioned heteronormativity and relationships and showed general ambiva-lence toward marriage. It is supposed to be a romantic ending—the guy who's been giving you the biggest runaround will finally come around and be what you want him to be—but it's actually disturbing since he's given her nothing but heartache, and has bordered on being emotionally abusive for most of their relation-ship. It tells us that ultimately we should settle for Mr. Very Ques-tionable, since there is no fairytale ending without a prince.

While *SATC* did open up space in pop culture for new ideas of what single life, sexuality, and romance for women might look like in a new generation, it only pushed us so far. The story lines in *SATC* speak to a mainstream brand of feminism that is predicated on a certain amount of capital wealth, independence, choice, and whiteness. It consolidated the rather problematic and unrealistic notion that independence is directly connected to wealth. Few of us have enough money to buy Manolo Blahniks or live the lifestyle of wealthy NYC socialites (or really even want that). The conclusion any reasonable person could draw from the show is that only a certain class of people have the luxury to make the kinds of choices the friends on *SATC* were able to make.

SATC also reinforced the age-old divide between race and sexuality, pushing forth the idea that only privileged white women have the right to "choose" single life, independence, and sexual freedom. It reinforced white standards of beauty, too, all the while ignoring the realities of race, class, and gender. Gay people and people of color were used to prop up the stories of white heterosexuality throughout the show, which is a trend in story lines about female sexual emancipation, but it was more troubling in *SATC*'s case since the purpose of the show was to break down how we understand sexuality.

SATC clearly wasn't ever as feminist as it could have been (it is, after all, popular culture and another kind of fairytale), and in many ways it reconsolidated popular myths of single life and heteronormativity. Yes, it's just television, not real life, but these stories occupy the popular imagination and impact how we actually think about the parameters of our own relationships. *SATC* was supposed to reflect the ethos of single womanhood for women in their thirties, reflecting the popular feminist sentiment of our day, but instead reinforced problematic myths about mainstream feminism, single life, and sexuality.

What Does "Single" Even Mean?

Popular culture suggests that single women are either abject failures deserving of our pity, à la reality TV, or complete "feminist" successes, à la *Sex and the City*. Popular myths about single life uphold unrealistic values that make actual real-life single women feel completely alienated. And while many will demand that being single is an absolutely legitimate lifestyle, women who are branded "single" are considered incomplete. Let's face it: We don't live in a world that is ready to accept, support, or represent single women in their totality.

The reality of being single is much more complex than Carrie Bradshaw. Single *and* married women are the fastest growing segment of the population when it comes to earnings. According to a 2010 study done by Prudential, women making over $50,000 have unprecedented spending power and are more financially responsible than ever before. Women in the United States today constitute over 50 percent of college students. And there have been significant improvements in the pay gap, too; single urban women earn more than their male counterparts. A study done in 2008 found that single childless women between the ages of twenty-two and thirty were earning more than their male counterparts in most U.S. cities, showing incomes on average greater than 8 percent.[2, 3]

But before you declare that sexism is over and the feminists won, it's important to note that women, on average, still earn less on the dollar than men. According to 2008 U.S. Census statistics, women still earned only seventy-seven cents to the male dollar. Black women earned only 68 percent and Latina women 58 percent of what their male counterparts earned.

And single life doesn't just look one certain way. It's profoundly different depending on your class, race, and gender, and on whether you are taking care of children. Of the 13.7 million single parents in the United States, 84 percent are mothers, and single women with children are more likely to be the primary caretaker. The "welfare mother" stereotype is generally overexaggerated, with only 27 percent of single mothers below the poverty line. However, these statistics change when you look at single black mothers, who constitute 3.1 million of the 10 million single mothers, and 38 percent of them live below the poverty line. For some women being single is a choice; for others it is a grave reality that puts them in one of the most vulnerable categories—at the greatest risk in the failing economy and often barely surviving in poverty. Single mothers who live in poverty have not scored the slew of benefits that the new, emancipated single woman has.

Single is diametrically opposed to marriage and therefore even its categorization upholds the idea that marriage is the standard, the future, and the inevitable. Part of the problem with the way being single exists in opposition to being married is that the multitude of ways people are living their lives gets ignored. Outside of social labels, "single" is a census category that means little more than lacking a piece of approval from the state, signatures, and a contract. Single just assumes unmarried; it doesn't assume multiple relationships, or boyfriends, co-parents, queer folks, single mothers, or any of the other plethora of ways that people live. As I discussed in Chapter 1, 45 percent of the adult population is unmarried, but that doesn't mean they are single per se, just not married. Assuming that single means "doing it on your own" invisiblizes alternative identities that are often non-heteronormative.

Now I know many single, successful women do want to get married, but the way this desire is characterized by the media is always couched in desperation and failure. This frame of failure obscures the reality that women are figuring out ways to do it all on their own without the support of traditional marriages and family structures. Women are supposed to have their primary reason for existence be marriage, so it is confusing when it is not. The notion that women shouldn't care about personal success—or the work that gets them there—is disingenuous; it is impossible for women not to have jobs anymore, so it doesn't make sense to expect them to structure their lives around getting married. The real failure is our cultural incapacity to make room for women to live and thrive outside of traditional conceptions of femininity and relationships. After all, we can eat without marriage, but not without work.

Single Women Are Too Picky

Despite the complexity of single women's actual lives, the media and relationship experts love to blame our "tragic" single status on us. Women are often chastised and blamed for their single status, as though we are dating in a vacuum and men don't exist. Tracy McMillan, a writer for *Mad Men,* wrote an article for *Huffington Post* titled, "Why You're Not Married," in which she detailed six reasons women are single: you're a bitch, you're shallow, you're a slut, you're a liar, you're selfish, you're not good enough.[4] Ironically, she is trying to give some "real talk" to the single ladies, but I think her list perfectly captures all of the hidden stories that inform popular culture and media myths about single women. We are constantly hated on and told we are too picky, too bitchy, that we lie about what we want, are selfish for putting our own needs first, and that we are not good enough—and all these reasons contribute to why we haven't found love yet. It's a pretty clever tactic to keep women unhappy and complicit in sexism to tell us that, after all our successes, we should be ashamed of ourselves for making men feel bad. And it's effective because women internalize these messages and spread these articles (like, *all* over Facebook).

The recurring media theme about the overabundance of single, unhappy, overeducated women tends to focus in on certain groups. The latest seems to be black women. In 2010, there were over a dozen news stories run by major outlets about how black women have gotten too successful, contributing to their inevitable path to singlehood—a story that even made it to *The Economist*. And the stories were framed as tragic; single black women are going to die alone and all the eligible black men are either gay, married, or in prison (you know how that story goes). In response to this trend, Steve Harvey and Jimi Izrael started giving unsolicited advice to black women about how their standards are too high, how black women's sense of entitlement has gone too far, and how they need to reel it in if they want to snag a man.[5]

In a special episode of *Nightline*, Jimi Izrael and Steve Harvey did a face-off with comedian Sherri Shepherd of *The View* fame about why so many successful single black women can't find a man. Izrael and Harvey both claimed emphatically that black wom-en have gotten too picky. Izrael said, "Women want someone per-fect, but you are not perfect." Shepherd retorted that she wants someone at the same level of success as herself, but Izrael and Harvey were unmoved. The crowd laughed, because who can get it through their thick skulls that after all our successes, we don't want to apologize for our success and would like to date men who aren't threatened by it. How that translates into women being too picky is beyond me.

It's not just Izrael and Harvey (two notoriously sexist and problematic authors) who have caught onto the "single women are too picky" meme. While they focus on black women in particular, there is no shortage of dating advice for all single, successful wom-en claiming that women today have gotten too picky. When I started writing this book, Lori Gottlieb's forget-feminism manifesto, *Marry Him: The Case for Settling for Mr. Good Enough*, was also getting a ton of press. In this book, Gottlieb takes the idea of settling to a new level by beating young women over the head with the idea that having high standards is not going to get you married. And with full recognition that the dating advice industry would reward her regressive attitudes on romance, she wrote a rather frustrated exposé about how she made a mistake by being too picky early in her life and now she's in her forties, single, and so not loving it.[6]

But, before I launch into what's problematic about encour-aging women to settle, I urge you to consider the male equivalent of Gottlieb's book. Can you imagine a book for men called *Marry Her: The Case for Settling for Ms. Good Enough*? No, of course not, because society doesn't put the same pressures on men to settle down. Period.

That said, Gottlieb's initial point is a good one; we should give worthy guys a chance. And sometimes women *are* unrealistic about what they are looking for, just like everyone is. And sometimes our defense mechanisms are high because we have been burned one too many times from our standards not being high *enough*. Most people are guilty of feeding into fantasies about what we are looking for in a partner. And there are, of course, awesome dudes out there who want to be in caring and supportive relationships, but again, the notion that women are responsible for spearheading the movement to coupledom is absurd and unfair. Men can have infinite standards, while women should settle.

Gottlieb, like other authors I discussed in the last chapter, posits her writing as the big aha to the dating industry because she threw in her figurative feminist towel, proclaiming that feminism ruined her love life and that trying to find happiness as a single woman was a mistake. The gender wars were right: If you want to get married, if you want to find partnership, if you want to find hetero-happiness, you better forget about those standards and that independence and get on the patriarchy train. Gottlieb caught onto something that many other so-called feminist authors have come to capitalize on: The mainstream media only pays attention to faux feminists who declare the key to romantic success is the death of their feminist ideals.

In Gottlieb's view, the type of guy it's okay to settle for includes "nice guys," like someone who might wear his pants too high or talk with food in his mouth. Most women I know would love a guy who's nice and perfect in every way other than his style. But most women's "settling" involves far more nefarious character flaws than the ones so flippantly addressed in *Marry Him*. If I am to be completely honest, most women's problem is not being picky enough. Many women are more generally settling for Mr. "I don't like to hang out with your friends," or Mr. "Yeah, feminism is cool, but, you know, I pretty much expect you to make dinner every night," or, in those worst-case scenarios, Mr. "I'm sorry I pushed you but it was just really that one time," or Mr. "It didn't mean anything with her—it's really *you* that I love." I mean, seriously, if one of my friends actually settled for someone whose biggest issue was wearing his pants too high I would give them a high-five (okay, maybe that's cheesy, but I would be really excited). Given that we live in a culture where women are too often complacent in abusive, unhappy, and oftentimes downright wrong relationships, suggesting that we should just settle is irresponsible.

Settling, which is essentially lowering your standards and expectations for yourself in the service of having a relationship, is what women have done for generations; it's something women have struggled and fought hard to not have to do anymore. Settling, after all, is what leads to high divorce rates, sexless marriages, cheating, and generally unhappy lives.

And I don't want to discredit the experience of Gottlieb and her generation of women who are frustrated about being single in their forties, but I would challenge her to ask herself whether her feelings might be a response to a sexist and patriarchal culture that lacks appropriate social support structures for single women over forty. I don't take issue with wanting to be in a relationship, but I do want to challenge her and anyone who agrees with her premise to consider what is an actual want versus the feeling that they *should* be in a relationship, and that if they were, they would be better, happier people, like their married friends.

It's important to note that people loved Gottlieb's book. Something about telling women to shut up and settle really sat well with people. It was a big hit and got featured in many progressive magazines. This was the dating book we had all ostensibly been waiting for. After all, it gets tiring when the super pro—family values ilk chastises women for being too choosy or faults them for being single. Here we have a feminist who lived the mainstream feminist dream, built her career, and even had children on her own—and for her it was terrible. Her unique life experience served to confirm the assumption that single women everywhere are as miserable as she is. Thanks for that, Lori.

The Feminist Potential of the Single Gal

Single as a "choice" is the holy grail of feminist self-preservation while single but "looking for love" puts you in the position of nonstop speculation as to why you can't find love. On an interpersonal level, when you are single, no one believes that you can be happy even when you say you are. Sometimes you begin to think, *Maybe I am not happy, and maybe my life is not fulfilling on my own.* Or sometimes, when you are sick of being single, you imagine people are thinking, *One day you will find what I've found* . . . (hey, misery loves company). But part of why we get to this place of self-pity in the first place is because the ideal we're supposed to be striving for is marriage, and without it we aren't living up to our full potential.

Being identified as single and having to juggle all the ideas put on you about your life can be very frustrating, especially when you add to it the pressure of everyone wondering why you are single, or your parents wanting you to find someone and settle down. You begin to feel like you should overcompensate and show off how amazing your life is, when at the end of the day it is just your life, you happen to be single, and there are things that are great about it and things that suck about it, just like any life, married or otherwise. And for most of us being single isn't *exactly* a choice, it just happened because we didn't meet someone we didn't want to not be single for.

And it's not like all single people are doing is sitting around waiting and hoping they can engage in the self-obliteration that is coupling. Perhaps the reason I loved *Sex and the City* so much was because I was longing for more mirroring of the position I am in as a single woman and for popular culture to showcase some of the nuances of single life. We are not always sad, lonely, pining for relationships, unlovable, food-obsessed, or vibrator queens (well, maybe sometimes we are one or more of these things at once or none of them—cough, vibrator queen, cough). It is nearly impossible to find images of single women as part of vibrant supportive communities, though that is where *most* people find their interpersonal relationship sustenance. And people forget, some of us like to be alone.

And yes, sometimes we get lonely, we get scared, we don't want to have babies alone, and we want to be in a relationship—and all of these experiences and feelings are just part of life, married, coupled, single, and otherwise. Of course being single can be lonely, but so can marriage. The frustrating outcome of the pressure single women feel to be in a relationship is that many women end up in unhappy relationships, and then they don't see leaving as an option because the thought of being alone is so horrifying to them. Being afraid of being alone, or even dying alone, is something most women can relate to, but there is tremendous power in overcoming that feeling. Feeling comfort with your single status, even if only sometimes, is an act of feminist self-preservation.

Being single is also a concrete act of resistance against hetero-patriarchy. I know you are thinking, *Why does my love life have to be part of that?*, but the more that single and unmarried people demand equal treatment in all settings, the more normalized this lifestyle and identity become. Statistically we are not outliers, we are the growing majority, so we should claim that ground. Part of the backlash against single women has to do with us being considered a threat to heteronormativity, to the economy, to social policy, and half the time to our friends' relationships. What better way to say fuck you to the system than by not kowtowing to other people's necessity for us to be coupled?

But single women can't do it alone; we need our coupled friends to help us. One of the ways we can fight sexism against single women is for couples, or rather anyone who directly benefits from heteronormativity, to recognize their couple privilege and start to open up about how they think about community and inclusion. It's time to rethink what we prioritize as legitimate social engagements and what types of relationships we privilege. Oftentimes people in relationships are so consumed in their monogamous lifestyle that they don't realize how they prioritize their lives around being coupled as opposed to being part of a broader community. Couples can start to make more of an effort to include single people in their lives and work toward pushing against the couple-centric structure of the world. While that may take courage and effort, it is one more step toward pushing against a society that demands heteronormative coupling for all people. We single gals are not going to be able to fight anti–single woman sexism without the support of our coupled sisters.

The fact of the matter is that being single is hard, and being in a relationship is hard, and most of us are going to vacillate between these two and many other relationship formations at different points in our lives. Granted, the pressure to be coupled is real, but as we get older we learn more about ourselves and the world around us. We start to make more informed choices about the kinds of partnerships we want and we start to see the joy in both single and coupled life. We are pickier about the relationships we become part of. These lessons are invaluable and can happen only when we have courage and take the opportunity to relish being on our own.

The most power I have gained from my single life is in the friendships I have with other women that have flourished in a noncompetitive environment where we don't prioritize our romantic relationships. Building powerful communities is the only way to keep us from being isolated in a world that wants to portray us as failures, to make us feel bad about our success, or to shame us for having pride. And since single women have nurtured their communities, we have people who take care of us. We laugh and enjoy our lives, go on vacations with friends, yes, often as a result of love or heartbreak, but for other reasons as well. Single women can't maintain their lifestyles alone, and when we go about it the right way, we don't have to.

NICE GUYS, PICKUP ARTISTS, and the MASCULINITY "CRISIS"

When we buy into the idea that female and male are "opposites," it becomes impossible for us to empower women without either ridiculing men or pulling the rug out from under ourselves.

—Julia Serano, *Whipping Girl*

{ CHAPTER SIX } In the summer of 2010, Cee-Lo's hit song "Fuck You!" hit the airwaves. The song is a bitter testimonial from Cee-Lo about a girl who broke his heart by leaving him for another man because he wasn't rich enough. The "fuck you" is mainly directed at the new boyfriend, but also to his ex. This song became a sort of national anthem for young men who were bitter about not being "man enough" to be with the women they wanted to be with. It became intensely popular, and with it came commentary (well, at least on Facebook) about how it was about time men speak out on their feelings of inadequacy about women, money, and romance. This declaration seemed justified given how much pressure men feel to provide in relationships (and given the state of the economy in 2010). It appeared more than ever that men were bitter about the pressure they're under to be a "man" today.

According to the mainstream media, masculinity is in a state of crisis. Men are not "men" anymore, because women are not "women" anymore. Women today go to college, have their own apartments, jobs, and their own money; they are no longer reliant on men for their financial needs (hypothetically). Meanwhile, the expectation for men to be the primary breadwinner, while unrealistic, is still encoded in our culture. These two competing stories, one of women's empowerment and the other of men being chivalrous manly men, have been characterized as a crisis, not of gender essentialism, but of manliness itself. The shift in actual gender disparity is quite slim, but the media circus that makes much ado about the whole thing would have you believing that men are the ultimate underdogs. As a result, men are receiving competing messages about what it means to be a man today, and the side effects include everything from anger and resentment to alienation and disaffectedness.

According to *The American Heritage Dictionary,* masculinity describes someone or something that possesses characteristics normally associated with males and can be "used to describe any human, animal, or object that has the quality of being masculine." Note that the dictionary definition asserts that there is a normal way to be male, but it does not make the mistake of connecting being male with being masculine.

We're all familiar with the standard understanding of masculinity. When we tell someone to "man up," we are drawing from conventional ideas of what it means to be a man—to be strong, unwavering, chivalrous, independent, together, and courageous. While none of these are bad characteristics, they suggest that masculinity is based on strength while femininity is based on weakness, ultimately limiting the way men and women are allowed to act and implying that those who act outside these norms are misfits, freaks, or, at the very best, outliers.

Only when we understand that masculinity, like femininity, is something we are taught, can we come to terms with the ways in which masculinity is socially constructed. Male-identified folks are hurt by unfair expectations to "be a man," and this form of gender essentialism is harmful across the board. The insistence to be a "man" and act in ways that are propagated by conventional ideas of manhood is implicated with violence (think bullying, prisons, sports, the military), repression (chastising little boys for liking "girly" things), and unfair expectations (men always have to pay, etc.) and often results in violence (intimate partner violence, sexual assault, etc.).

The burden put on men to be "men," the shifting nature of women's roles, and the overstated crisis in masculinity have had three side effects: (1) it has conflated female success with male failure; (2) it has exaggerated the actual success that women have made (both in the world and in romance); and (3) it has led to angry and/or disaffected male behavior. I have talked throughout this book about the pressures women feel to act a certain way in romance and love, and the purpose of this chapter is to show how unfair expectations of men hurt both men and women.

Deconstructing the Masculinity "Crisis"

If you turn on the television, read a newspaper, or listen to the radio, you'd be led to believe that men are now second-class citizens and completely disenfranchised. The supposed crisis in masculinity is everywhere you look, from men's rights activists (a small, but very loud minority of men whose primary issues include alimony and custody, but who also manage to say appalling things about women's rights) to progressive authors. According to its proponents, the crisis is affecting men and boys starting from elementary school—aged kids and impacting men in college, the workplace, and the domestic sphere. According to critics, men are the ones supposedly worst hit by the collapsing economy.

David Brooks writes in *The New York Times* that we're living in a "woman's world" in response to the shift in women's roles. He writes, "The social consequences are bound to be profound. The upside is that by sheer force of numbers, women will be holding more and more leadership jobs. On the negative side, they will have a harder and harder time finding marriageable men with comparable education levels. One thing is for sure: in 30 years the notion that we live in an oppressive patriarchy that discriminates against women will be regarded as a quaint anachronism."[1] Brooks, similar to many of his "men are in crisis" contemporaries, equates female success with male failure, and even goes as far as to suggest that women's progress has been so steady that patriarchy will cease to exist in thirty years!

I can only hope that Brooks's predication about the end of patriarchy is right, but his assertions about the declining power of men have been overstated. As I mention in the last chapter, women overall still make less money than men, nationwide. They still own less property. They still get booted from jobs for getting pregnant or are still fighting for fair maternity leave. And while women in many cases are better educated than men, they still make less money (often in the same positions).[2]

As much as I disagree with his assessment, it's not just the conservative camp that's spouting off this kind of rhetoric. The shift in traditional gender roles has irked even some progressive writers. Hanna Rosin's much talked about 2010 piece in *The Atlantic*, "The End of Men," notes that we are in a new phase of social and economic order and the rapid success of women in the workplace shows us that the times they are a-changin'. Rosin suggests that perhaps the evolutionary psychologists were wrong: It's not a biological imperative that demands men work in aggressive, competitive fields and women at home or in pink-collar jobs; it's social pressure and economic need that has put men and women in these roles. She poses some important questions: "What if that era has now come to an end? More to the point, what if the economics of the new era are better suited to women?"[3] According to this argument, jobs have changed and skills that are considered feminine are more in demand—specifically communication skills, efficiency in office tasks, and multitasking—and Rosin's claim is that since women are better at these things, they are more successful in the workplace and in life.

While Rosin is right to question evolutionary psychology and its sweeping generalizations about "natural" characteristics in men and women that have worked to establish the foundation for men's and women's roles in society, she still gets caught in the gender essentialism trap. The assumption that certain skills are for women and others are for men ignores how men and women are socialized to excel in certain roles. We are taught from a very young age that certain skills and characteristics are masculine while others are feminine, and then we are pummeled with constant messaging based on our sex as to which of these roles we should be fulfilling.

The problem with the "masculinity crisis" is not that women have excelled too much and therefore created a crisis for men, but that we have such a strong inability to let go of what it has traditionally meant to be a man. In response to Rosin's piece, Ann Friedman at *The American Prospect* writes, "She thinks the problem is men; really, it's traditional gender stereotypes. The narrow, toxic definition of masculinity perpetuated by Rosin and others—that men are brawn not brains, doers not feelers, earners not nurturers—is actually to blame for the crisis."[4] As long as we perpetuate the myth that men have inherent qualities that make them more suitable than women for certain types of work, the shifting nature of the economy (and women's attainment of better and better jobs) is going to continue to be interpreted as a crisis of masculinity.

Lest you think this crisis in masculinity is new, think again. In her newest book, *A Strange Stirring: The Feminine Mystique and American Women at the Dawn of the 1960s*, Stephanie Coontz finds multiple points in history where a masculinity crisis arose. In an interview, she told *Salon*'s Tracy Clark-Flory, "People have been proclaiming a 'masculinity crisis' since the 1890s and, actually, it's very interesting that when you go back to the 1940s and '50s, a lot of the vitriol directed at women was because they thought there was a 'masculinity crisis' at that time. The idea was that domineering women in the home were expecting too much of their husbands and were driving them to work too many hours."[5] What Coontz describes is not so different from what we're seeing today, in that it's women's emancipation and supposed lack of reliance on or need for men's support that have called into question the very definition of masculinity.

The truth is that masculinity has been in crisis for a long time, but it has nothing to do with women being threatening. It has to do with the fact that masculinity is a constructed fallacy to begin with. Men and women have always worked together in multiple, creative, and diverse ways for survival and convenience. Gender roles have shifted throughout history depending on political, economic, and social circumstances, and despite this the push for traditional gender roles has prevailed.

What it means to be a man also varies across race and class. Historically, working-class women have always had to work, and men from disenfranchised backgrounds (gay, immigrant, men of color, incarcerated populations, differently abled, trans) have never benefited from the privileges of being a conventional man. Yes, masculinity has been in crisis for a long time, but it's only now starting to be paid attention to because it's impacting middle-class white men.

And what are the subliminal messages we're sending out when we propagate the message that female success is ruining traditional ideas of masculinity? It suggests that women should stay in "their place." It suggests that women should have not been given access to jobs and education, as this disrupts normal ideals of masculinity. And it suggests that the only way men can feel comfortable is when women are inferior to them. The rhetoric also assumes that in order to be a man you must be better than a woman, echoing traditional ideas of masculinity that are predicated on the belief that men are superior to women.

The most serious implication of the rhetoric, however, is the ways in which it impacts pay equity legislation, reproductive rights, and other types of legislation that guarantee women basic civil liberties to protect their bodies, communities, and families. Suggesting that men are in crisis brings into question the very rights that feminists have fought to earn for women, while neglecting to build any space for men to express or explore the shifting nature of masculinity.

The idea that female empowerment equals male disempowerment puts women in a position where they feel like they have to downplay their successes for the benefit of the male ego. Often, women become afraid to claim their successes for fear they will not meet a man who wants to be with them for the long-term. Remember, lots of women are afraid to even ask men out. Similarly, men either feel like they have to overcompensate or feel embarrassed by their lack of success.

While the crisis in masculinity has been overstated, there have been some concrete shifts in how men and women date, but this is always characterized in the media as a negative trend. Trend pieces invariably decry the decline or loss of femininity while upholding conventional ideas of masculinity. They highlight how giving up sex too early hurts your chances at romance; how men are intimidated by female success; how all the good men are gone; and how specific subgroups of women are single because of their career success.

One example of this "trend" can be seen in a fall 2010 *New York Times* article titled "Keeping Romance Alive in the Age of

Female Empowerment," by Katrin Bennhold. On first glance you wonder if it is an *Onion* headline, but no, Bennhold actually states the case for why women should downplay their accomplishments in an effort to foster "romance." Per usual, romance and female empowerment are diametrically opposed to each other. The author concludes, "Leave the snazzy company car at home on the first date; find your life partner in your 20s, rather than your 30s, before you've become too successful."[6] According to writers like Bennhold, men are fragile flowers who are easily intimidated by your success, so hide it, and while you are at it, hide who you are as well. Get married in your twenties, because when you're old (and successful) no one is going to like you. The picture this paints of women is bleak and the assumption it makes about men is disgraceful.

It's easy to ignore such an obviously outdated article about gender roles, but the reality is that the author is taking her cues from current themes about men, women, and romance. In a piece for *TBD.com*, Amanda Hess writes about the gender essentializing nature of these types of articles and how they "make light of our most basic identities as women—they tell us how our civil rights are ruining our interpersonal relationships, how our wombs are interfering with our higher education, and whether our basic body types are currently socially acceptable."[7] When *The New York Times*, one of the main purveyors of cultural trends, publishes story after story that are based on sexist attitudes toward men and women, we should be concerned. Due to its reach, these stories become talking points and impact how the public thinks about romance, female empowerment, and masculinity.

The cultural reluctance to let go of what it means to be a

man is most obvious in the onslaught of "death of masculinity" flavored media. But the crisis is not an actual shift; it is more a reflection of the anxieties facing a changing world. These anxieties have made themselves known through an increasingly angry male youth culture, as seen in popular culture with violent video games and music, disaffected male culture (Judd Apatow anyone?), or in more obscure places, like men's rights groups and the pickup art scene. What is often ignored in the "crisis" of masculinity is that male dominance in most arenas hasn't actually shifted *that* much, which suggests that many of these side effects are driven by false information, insecurity, and a media saturated with conflicting images of what it means to be a man today.

Man-boys

One response to the tensions arising between men not living up to the "manly man" expectation and women striving to be empowered superwomen has been the emergence of a new type of man—the perpetually childlike man-boy who is sitting on a couch near you smoking weed, drinking beers, and playing video games. This man-boy deals with his perceived inadequacy by deciding he doesn't have to be in a serious relationship, and as a result, he never has to grow up. This man-boy loves his friends before he loves the ladies ("bromance" anybody?), he has enough expendable income to do whatever he wants (mostly), and, well, smoking that much weed makes you pretty damn unmotivated anyway. This dude, the character featured in Judd Apatow movies, is sensitive about his lack of aggressive masculinity. He is insecure, isn't very serious about life, and doesn't really have to be.

The existential battles of the nerdy, nice, dorky dude, at first glance in movies like *The 40-Year-Old Virgin, Knocked Up,* or *Superbad* (all hilarious), seem to disrupt traditional conceptions of masculinity, since they characterize men as more sensitive, disorganized, less methodical, and not that physically attractive. They are "nice guys" who have been wronged by life and women. But upon closer examination we see that these don't give alternative models of masculinity per se. They do not display nicer, more compassionate, or less sexist behavior toward women; all women are cast as moms or babes, obstacles to overcome or objects of sexual desire. The movies, in fact, highlight men's failures—failures hidden behind fart jokes, broken careers, and running from the accountability of real relationships (from needy, often shrill, but totally together women). Man-boys are characterized as failures of masculinity, but somehow continue to benefit from male privilege—because, well, they are still men.

Women who want to be dating from this subset of (mostly fictional) men are far from satisfied. In her book, *Manning Up: How the Rise of Women Has Turned Men into Boys,* Kay Hymowitz makes the case that the rise of female empowerment has destabilized masculinity and that there are no "men" left. In a *Wall Street Journal* piece titled "Where Have the Good Men Gone?" Hymowitz sees men acting like boys as, "an expression of our cultural uncertainty about the social role of men. It's been an almost universal rule of civilization that girls became women simply by reaching physical maturity, but boys had to pass a test. They needed to demonstrate courage, physical prowess, or mastery of the necessary skills. The goal was to prove their competence as protectors and providers. Today, however, with women moving ahead in our advanced economy, husbands and fathers are now optional, and the qualities of character men once needed to play their roles—fortitude, stoicism, courage, fidelity—are obsolete, even a little embarrassing."[8] Hymowitz, a known conservative writer, might be overstating how much progress women have actually made, but her anxiety is a common one: Where *have* all the good men gone?

What is overlooked in these frustrated gasps of romantic dreams unrealized is that by asking where have the "men" gone, we are feeding into toxic and traditional ideas of masculinity. It's true, both on-screen and in real life, man-boys don't go far enough in disrupting the ethos of masculinity to present us with an alternative male psychology. This is what prompts the question in the first place, but the anxiety and idea that there are no "good men" left stems from fictitious ideas of men. Jill Filipovic writes at *Feministe,* in response to Hymowitz's description of the man-boy, "Maybe I'm hanging out at the wrong bars, but far more common is the twenty- or thirty-something dude (or lady) who has a wide variety of interests, a job he's okay with but an eye for something better, a wide social network and few external pressures to settle for less than what he really wants, in love or family or career. He might also watch Comedy Central and enjoy a good dick joke and a beer every now and again. And you know, that describes me too. It's actually pretty great. Dick jokes are funny. Good beer tastes good." Man-boys are as much media constructed fallacies as desperate educated single women are. Yeah sure, there are a few of them and all of us share some of the anxieties these media constructions capture, but for the most part they don't actually represent us in our totality.[9]

For most men, the characterization of men as "boys," due

to not hurrying through conventional markers of adulthood, is harsh. It's an almost feminist-style chastising of single men, but it's ultimately just reconsolidating gender essentialism. Similar to Filipovic, in my experience, a lot of the men that might be cast as man-boys are not that different from me—they are figuring things out in a world that's constantly changing. The ones who want to be in relationships are in relationships and will be irrelevant of their financial status or their supposed freedom not to have to be in a relationship. And men who respect women and are accountable to their feelings were like that in the first place, and a shifting economy is not going to change who they are.

Also, Filipovic points out something that the Apatow movies and Hymowitz have failed to capture—all women aren't parading around yelling at men to man-up so they can have their babies. A lot of women are also taking advantage of a new world in which marriage doesn't happen immediately, and where taking the time to figure out what we want with our lives and careers before we settle down is a good thing. If the supposed crisis in masculinity has shown us anything, it's that the more natural course of action is to allow for gender to shift with the changing social, economic, and political climate, as opposed to demanding we regress to more traditional gender roles.

The Art of Womanizing: Pickup Artists and the Seduction Community

The responses to the feelings of insecurity that have transpired due to the masculinity crisis run the gamut from the less nefarious rise of "man-boys" to vivid displays of misogyny (as can be seen by the men's rights activists and other ardent angry decriers of the new vagina overlords) to the less violent but just as toxic rise in men's dating advice that tells men how to be pickup artists.

Pickup art, or the art of seduction, has been pushed through books, classes, seminars (full-on very expensive retreats), and websites that tell men that they need to use certain psychological tactics to get women to have sex with them. The purpose of pickup art, supposedly, is to support men with their self-esteem. But if you've ever survived the advances of a pickup artist, you know that their only purpose is to manipulate women's insecurities in an effort to get laid. Pickup artists acknowledge power differentials between men and women and then come up with clever and creative ways to manipulate them.

The bible of pickup art for our generation is Neil Strauss's *The Game: Penetrating the Secret Society of Pickup Artists*. A quick glance at the chapters gets you familiar with the language and mind-set of pickup art, including Chapter 1, "Select a Target," Chapter 5, "Isolate the Target," Chapter 6, "Create an Emotional Connection," Chapter 7, "Extract to a Seduction Location," Chapter 10, "Blast Last-Minute Resistance," and finally, Chapter 11, "Manage Expectations." This kind of language tells us that men are hunters, women are their game, and the ladies men should be trying to connect with are nothing but targets for the purpose of sex.[10] Unfortunately, it also sounds like a manual for date rape.

I perused a few pickup artist websites, too, and found a wide variety of information, from less nefarious advice on how to be confident to violent language about women. One website, "Pickup Art Mindset," tells guys what to do when a woman responds poorly to "using a line":

*"If a girl accuses you of using a line . . . she's not going to
fuck you. It simply won't happen. . . . Chances are she came
out to make men feel small and get free drinks, so therefore
you must go over the top and put that bitch in her place. . . .
Say: 'Well it got me laid last week with some slut. I don't see
why it shouldn't work again.' Enjoy the embarrassed look on
her face as she stews in silence trying to think of a come-
back. Then turn your back on her. She'll think twice before
saying that nonsense to another man."*[11]

I think this extract speaks for itself.

Most pickup art proponents will tell you that it's not all
about hate and anger toward women; it's about helping men with
their self-esteem. Of course, healthy self-esteem is a good thing.
It helps you ask people out, and not be overly offended if you are
rejected. I'm sure the majority of guys drawn to these books, websites, and communities are probably decent guys with social anxiety and a real desire to connect with women, and I sympathize
with that need and genuinely support actual real-world nice guys
to get that help.

But none of the pickup artist materials I've seen support the
self-esteem hypothesis, and they don't teach men to connect authentically with women. They teach them instead how to control
women. Tactics include jabbing at women (called a "neg," short
for negative remark, a.k.a., an insult couched in a compliment,
like making a comment about how she looks that seems nice but
actually plays on her insecurities). Or playing games, like showing
interest in her, but not too much interest, for the purpose of keeping her wondering and captivated. Another tactic is "kino-ing"
(kino is short for kinesthetics), which means touching someone
to make the situation comfortable.

Most of the message boards and websites dedicated to pick-up art are full of trolls decrying their hatred for women, all the while professing what "nice guys" they are and how they still can't get women to have sex with them. Anyone who claims he is a nice guy and therefore women should automatically have sex with him probably isn't really a nice guy. In a lot of instances it appears "nice guys" believe they are nice because they don't physically abuse women or yell at them, or because they opened a door or paid for a meal. This, of course, should give them an all-access pass to vagina park, but since it doesn't, some of them are very very angry.

Perhaps a lot of these guys are all bark and no bite, but the dark side of the pickup community is that it glorifies misogynistic displays of power. From there it's a slippery slope to committing crimes of coercion and violence against women. One pickup artist in Israel posted details of a recent date on a message board, citing tactics learned in *The Game*. Scarily, his description of the event sounded like a date rape, excerpted here from the Israel/Palestine based political blog *972*:

> "Things moved along . . . believe me, I came across count-less objections on the way to close an FC [fuck close], but I persisted and stayed consistent to the end. Okay we started making out on the bed and she just refused to take off her clothes and made all kinds of excuses . . . but I'm a blind rhino, she doesn't know me. I used a quick seduction technique and it totally confused her. I took her hand and put it on my cock . . . slowly slowly I closed a BJC [blowjob close]."[12]

In this case, "blasting last-minute resistance" means forcing her into having sex.

Two recent examples of pickup artists who went on to commit violent crimes toward women are Allen Robert Reyes, known as "Gunwitch," who shot a woman in the face at a party in January of 2011,[13] and George Sodini, who opened fire in a Pittsburgh gym. He targeted women, at random, and killed three of them.[14] Yes, these are extreme examples and don't reflect the majority of men who participate in pickup art communities, but they are telling of a particular attitude reflected in the language of these communities. There is a relationship between feelings of rejection from women and the desire to control them, whether through violence or psychology.

I asked feminist/masculinity studies writer and teacher Hugo Schwyzer if, from his perspective, pickup art communities can be good for men. His response was, "Yes, in the sense that unhealthy fast food is better than starvation to someone who hasn't eaten in a week. But it doesn't address the root cause of so many men's sense that they are losers in the sexual economy. It promises so much more than it delivers. . . . " It's unfortunate that men feel insecure about talking to women and when they go to find out what to do about it they find advice about how to control women, as opposed to learning how to respect and love them (and themselves).

Seduction isn't inherently bad. Flirting and sexual tension are some of the most pleasurable parts of dating. The dance of meeting someone and the buildup of sexual tension that follows is exciting and can be extremely satisfying.

But there is a difference between someone who hits on you because they think you are sexy, smart, and awesome, and someone who sees you as a target to be controlled and willed into sexual submission. Pickup art is not about propping women up, supporting their sexuality, or having equal relationships; it's about control and manipulation, plain and simple.

I have been "picked up" twice by guys who were trying the art of seduction on me. In both instances, I thought they were friendly and interesting at first, until they started making bizarre and personal comments and touching my shoulder. One even went so far as to say the girl he was supposed to meet that night was someone he had no "spark" for. (I suggested he tell her so.) I was confused by their actions in both cases, and in both cases the men were confused when I didn't fall for their games. So it led me to the hypothesis that (feminism+self-esteem) x (pickup artist+corny lines) = pickup art dating system failure.

Moving to a New Model of Masculinity

The reason men so often benefit in the sexual economy of romance isn't because women are too successful. It also isn't because men don't want to be in relationship, or because we have lost a traditional sense of what relationships should be. It is because sexism is still alive and thriving. Male self-esteem isn't bound by the success of men's relationships, but rather their financial status, sexual bravado, and how often they can get laid. And often what is hidden behind that bravado is a whole lot of insecurity. I know what it is like to date the cheater, the player, the self-hater, the misogynist, and the disaffected dudes. I've dated them all. But deep down, I've come to see how these behaviors all mask low self-esteem, an inability to adapt to a changing world, and difficulty navigating what it means to be a man.

If men are no longer providers, where is their self-esteem going to come from? While women may not always need the financial support of men, what we do need more than anything is the emotional support of men in our romantic relationships. Sadly, this is one thing traditional masculinity is not good at teaching young men how to do: to deal with their emotions around romance and sexuality. So instead of looking at external factors based in sexist assumptions of what it means to be a man—like lack of solid income, career goals, and ability to commit—we should be thinking about what young men need to support themselves and the women in their lives emotionally. It seems like many men are opting out of traditional ideas of masculinity, but what is the non-man-boy alternative?

A few months ago, my brother—who for many years was the quintessential "man-boy"—said something to me that really impacted the way I understood how men are dealing with this shifting idea of what it means to be a man. In previous years, he said, he thought being a man meant being unaccountable to women and ignoring their feelings. Looking back, he realized he'd abused his male privilege and acted selfishly in his relationships. In the last few years, he has made a concerted effort to be more accountable to women, even if just to tell them he was not interested. He changed the way he interacted with women to take the time to be responsible and share how he felt, listening and being as supportive as possible. This, he said, is what it really means to be a man, and part of his process was to unlearn what he had been taught it meant to be a man.

I was proud of my brother for reaching this conclusion and making such a serious effort to consciously change how he was relating to women, and this conversation opened my eyes to the damage that has been done to the psyche of male-identified folk by masculinity. Part of the reasoning behind calling the shift in masculinity a crisis is that it's about uncovering this age-old conspiracy that men don't have feelings. Rather than expose those feelings and the history of neglect and abuse that comes with it, it is much easier to suggest that being disaffected, abusive, unemotional, and disconnected is actually the natural way of being a man.

If men are still judged by external factors, like how much money they make, how nicely they dress, how tall they are, and how disconnected they can be from women, emotional dudes who don't have high-paying jobs are not going to feel too good about themselves. When men are effeminate and chastised for it, this feeds into regressive ideas of masculinity and puts unfair pressure on men to act a certain way. Homophobic and sexist epithets are used to bully men of all ages into conforming to a rigid idea of what it means to be a man. All of these conditions indicate that we are lacking alternative models in masculinity.

Furthermore, women internalize these messages and they often expect their partners to be a certain way, not realizing how this expectation supports the very structure that keeps them stuck in rigid gender binaries. The worst impact of this is that it may lead men to act out violently, generally toward their intimate partners.

We are hardly living in a post-sexist culture. Male privilege is alive and thriving. But men have undue pressure on them to be studs and to act a certain way toward women as well. Until we redefine masculinity, we have to take a more radical and compassionate approach to dating. And it will take both men and women to shift the ways they think about the role of men and masculinity. For women, most of the time that means walking away when we are not getting what we need, or shifting our expectations in our relationships and working toward a conversation that allows for new and experimental types of masculinity. For men, it means thinking about how they benefit from male privilege, where they get their self-validation, and pushing themselves to think about emotional accountability and how they view women and relationships. Wishful thinking? Maybe. But it's a good place to start.

DATING
WHILE FEMINIST
(DWF)

All reaction is limited by, and dependant on, what it is reacting against.
—Gloria Anzaldúa

{ CHAPTER SEVEN } As feminist women, perhaps we can take comfort in realizing that much of the pressure we feel is fabricated by the romance industry. It is, of course, depressing that such an industry exists in the first place, but if we stay conscious, we can see that whatever our romantic status is, it is not as tragic or desperate as some would like us to believe. Once we realize the ways in which we're pummeled with messaging around dating, we can let go of some of the heaviness of it all and think about what we really want (and have some fun!). After all, many of us want to be in relationships, whether casual or serious. So we need to ask ourselves a few questions: How do we date as feminists in a world that is so structured around patriarchy, power, and privilege? How do we create lasting alliances when men and women are pitted against each other? And how do we find happiness when pressure and social expectation dictate so much of how we should engage romantically?

These are some really big questions to tackle when sometimes your only goal might be going out and getting laid, or having a drink followed by a make-out session. While these three questions are ones I've been working to untangle throughout this book, our responses to each of them are going to vary a lot from person to person. And this book is not about finding answers per se, but rather to help women sort out the best ways to navigate the existing romantic terrain.

What is often lost in conversations about dating, romance, and feminism is some of the nuance around how we interact with one another when we actually do date. Not everyone we date is going to be 100 percent feminist and not every feminist dating scenario is going to feel 100 percent feminist. For me, a bigger question has been how do I draw the line for what is and isn't acceptable behavior—for myself, my friends, and the people I date—without being overly dogmatic about what feminism means when it comes to romance?

Throughout this book, I have touched upon the idea of an in-between space—what I often refer to as a third space—where most of our relationships are happening. This is a place that exists in between "single" or "in a committed monogamous relationship." Those of us who are not completely coupled and not completely single are engaging romantically all the time, and many of us will be living in this third space for our entire adult lives. You might characterize this third space as the sphere of "dating"— complete with breakups, times of being single, and times of being in serious relationships. Ultimately, though, this in-between space is scary, full of pitfalls and conundrums. For a space that's teeming with so much potential, dating sucks—and it's time for us to talk about why.

Hopeless Romantic or Glutton for Punishment?

How many times has it happened? You make a date with someone, whether through an Internet dating service, a friend, or someone you meet in real life. You get excited because they're cute, interesting, maybe they wear cool glasses. You both love that obscure band you thought no one had heard of. After becoming friends on Facebook, you discover that you both like the same HBO shows and have more similar tastes in music, books, and movies. You immediately start to think about all the awesome conversations you are going to have over your favorite music and really good guacamole (at least this is what's going on in my head).

So you contact them and you wait; you are totally psyched about what the future holds. *Sex,* you are thinking, *I am going to have sex!* The first few text messages are exciting. There's still the mystery of where this all could lead (and as veteran and conscientious romantics, we are very careful not to put *too* much pressure on it, but just enough to be hopeful).

Unfortunately, the majority of the time it doesn't go the way you hoped it would, and all that potential goes out the window.

Either you don't hit it off, or you find out they are already in a relationship, or you go out a few times and then they stop contacting you, or you just lose interest. In the best-case scenario, you make a new friend. But who needs more friends when what you really want is a lover? And despite the disproportionate number of times dating leads to disappointment instead of happiness, drama rather than calm, a waste of time instead of a fulfilling investment, we do it again. And what's more, we are *excited* to do it again.

Are we avid daters hopeless romantics or gluttons for punishment? Or maybe both? For most of us, dating sucks. I'm not talking about you world-class dating aficionados who maintain high self-esteem and a totally positive outlook. You go on with your badass self and healthy attitude. I'm talking about the rest of us heartbroken, hopeless romantics who are disappointed every time we try and try and fail (yes, this is getting a little bit personal).

Sure, sometimes dating can be fun, but the whole notion of going through a series of interviews to meet the "person of your dreams" and settle down is a torturous process. I go through periods where I think I love dating, but then I look back on the not-so-great dates I may have had in the last few months and I think, *wow, was all that really necessary?* If it wasn't guessing games, it was feelings of rejection, or meeting one more person that you *should* like, but you just don't though you can't figure out why. Maybe it was getting your hopes up only to be let down, and before you know it you are depressed about being single even though just the week before you were riding high on your single status.

Most public discourse about "feminist dating" focuses on rather unimportant and obvious questions like splitting the bill, opening the doors, or who makes the first move. But what about more substantive questions like how to deal with your emotions and desires as a feminist-minded person, or how your emotions and desires correlate with what is expected of you based on your gender?

As someone who engages romantically (if you will) on a regular basis with people of varying backgrounds and interests, I frequently stumble into confusing situations, and when I turn toward my feminism for guidance, often it's come up short. While I have spent most of this book deconstructing the structural, social, political, economic, and popular culture barriers to "dating," I have talked little about the interpersonal choices, connections, moments, and frustrations that we face on a regular basis when trying to "date while feminist" (DWF). In my adventures of DWF, I have tried just about everything, from open relationships to strictly casual encounters to regular heteronormative "dating."

According to conventional standards, I am a total dating failure. I am single, unmarried, and without a family at the ripe old age (har har) of thirty-three. But, as Cornel West says, "Of course it's a failure. But the real question is 'how good a failure is it?'"[1] Well, it's been an excellent failure and I have fared and failed well. Like any other romantically inclined person, I have faced heartbreak, obsession, happiness, sadness, longing, satisfaction, and all the other emotions that come along with opening yourself up to someone else. I have had deep connections (sexual and otherwise) with people and uncovered truths that may have been obscured had I limited myself to the sole goal of finding a husband and having kids.

In writing this book, my aim has not been solely to critique conventional and problematic dating practices that leave many of us disappointed and unhappy; rather, I have tried to illuminate and offer the alternative spaces that are so under wraps and un-acknowledged that they are difficult to find even for people who are desperately looking for them. Those of us daters trying to find our way in a world that wants to force us into specific relationship molds are both hopeless romantics and gluttons for punishment, because even when we fail, we keep trying.

Ten Things I Hate about Dating

1. *You are expected to dress nice and act a certain way while "waiting" to get asked out.*
2. *You have to play by the rules (wait till he calls you, don't be too forward, be mysterious, you don't want to scare him off, etc.), which generally give men most of the power.*
3. *If you show emotion too early on, or too much of it, you are needy.*
4. *If you don't show enough emotion, you are making the other party insecure, forcing them to wield social privilege to silence your daring attempt at independence from self-obliteration via coupling.*
5. *It fetishizes unequal power relations between men and women. (He'll get the tab, or the door, as long as he gets the vagina.)*
6. *It reinforces the gender binary.*
7. *It dictates your interaction in most social settings and social circles, whether you are single or coupled. It is either/or; there is no third identity or in-between.*
8. *If you have sex too early you ruined it.*
9. *If you don't have sex early on you are a prude.*
10. *It is expected to lead to marriage (and if you don't have a ring on your finger you are "on the market").*

A Little Rejection Never Killed Anybody

Dating advice is generally misguided because it doesn't take into account how our lives have changed and if it does it chastises us for it. Most dating books hinge on the idea that traditional gender roles haven't changed and that all men are hunters who need to catch their prey and all women are passive recipients waiting to be caught. Biology and history have shown us that there is much more variance in mating than the hunter/prey narrative allows for, and that the majority of us are a little hunter and a little prey. (Yes, I'm saying we are all a little top and all a little bottom.) And what we prefer may or may not match up to what's expected of us based on our gender. Most dating advice draws from a structure and style of relationships that doesn't apply to contemporary people who are juggling multiple aspects of their life at once— dating being just one of them.

In Chapter 4, I talked about the commonly held sexist dating myth that women should never ask a guy out. It's obvious why this is a sexist standard, but it is also a feminist dating conundrum. This unfair double standard challenges even the most feminist-minded of daters because it is not just about who should have the right to ask whom out, it is also about how power plays out in dating.

In my experience, as someone who is extremely outgoing and knows what I want, I like to make the first move. I know I can be intimidating, but in my opinion it's better to let someone know I'm interested rather than play the game. But, as I talked about earlier, it took me a while to get to this place. You have to come to terms with the fact that you might get rejected. For me, it took getting feedback from guys that they were flattered but not necessarily interested that allowed me to feel like I had nothing to lose. And it was realizing that most things worth doing take courage and a little bit of risk.

But it's not easy. It takes work to know that I might be rejected and then to find ways to overcome the embarrassment that might come if I am! Rejection, after all, is bound up in the way we see ourselves as women; because of internalized and social pressure, getting positive attention from men is tied to our self-esteem. Asking a guy out, therefore, is almost an act of defiance to a larger power structure that dominates our desires and our self-worth. You are saying to yourself, and the world, that you are willing to be rejected because you know that your self-worth is not determined by how a man responds to you.

The reason outdated advice that tells women not to ask men out bothers me so much is because it creates a power differential in which the men get to decide who they want to date while the women sit around waiting, passive and hopeful. As it stands, men have the social backing and power to say no and to determine the terms of the relationship. There is an implicit understanding that there is an endless surplus of women who want to be in relationships, so the stakes are higher when women are rejected.

Does that mean that men feel equally rejected—to the point that it's connected to their self-worth—when they make the first move and are turned down? Absolutely. Their egos get bruised and they too fear dying alone, just like women do. My roommate Puck told me, "Well, first I agonize over whether a woman might reject me, and then I have to convince myself that I will be okay if she says no, so I can at least get myself to ask." My best friend

Dave admitted, "Every time I want to ask someone out I have to silence my inner critic. If I think someone I am interested in asking out might not like me, I look for evidence to the contrary and remind myself of that when I get nervous." Another friend told me he gets so scared that he never asks women out. Men and women share common insecurities around rejection and romance. Often, we reject ourselves before the other person does through our own feelings of insecurity. We say no to ourselves before asking the potential object of our interests.

Women technically have as many choices as men do when it comes to dating, but we are not taught that we do. We are taught that if we are not pretty enough, we won't get a date, and that we only have a certain amount of time before we "expire." And then there's the ongoing mainstream media conversation about the shortage of men (covered in Chapter 5). It's not as easy to just say across the board this is a function of social conditioning; it has to do with both social conditioning and self-esteem. There are many men who don't feel good-looking enough, or rich enough, or successful enough to date. But whether we're talking about men or women, these are cultural standards that we internalize, not actual truths.

Some of the most confident of feminist daters I know will tell you that sometimes, even though they know they could ask a guy out, they don't because they can tell it would disrupt the expected flow of gender dynamics, and they're worried that the guy would lose interest before anything even got off the ground. We engage in annoying games like these based on ideas we know are sexist because we feel like we have to.

And there is a reason we feel like we have to play these

games. While the guys I asked seemed comfortable with women asking them out, there are guys who have not shed their internalized sense of masculinity enough to be truly comfortable with a woman making the first move. And it is not just about control; men have also internalized the belief that they will be less of a man if they do not have the ability or togetherness to make the first move. And many women have not shed the idea that equates making the first move with being a real man. I would even go as far as to say this power struggle may not be intentional or conscious, but rather is a side effect of internalizing and benefiting from power differentials that cast us in roles that we literally "play."

As responsible feminist daters, the only games we should be playing are the ones that we want to play (in the bedroom or otherwise), not the ones we feel like we have to. There are plenty of guys who would dig being asked out—shy guys, nice guys, feminist guys, and more. So just do it—ask him out. A little rejection won't kill you. You have nothing to lose, but so much to gain.

Passionate Connections, Dysfunctional Dynamics

You *know* the types of relationships that are totally unstable and dysfunctional. We've all experienced them. He disappears and reappears, you only see each other at 4:00 AM on Saturday, he forgets about your date, he is not accountable to you in any concrete way, but you forgive him every time he shows up. You are not accountable to him either, but the sex is really good, so what the hell. And he is genuinely sweet (no, really, he's actually a really great guy), but for whatever reason he is never around and you are just kind of letting it happen. After all, you are busy, you have other things going on, and you don't want that kind of traditional, conventional relationship anyway and there are things that are great about the connection. It makes you feel alive. The relationship is like a drug: When it's good it's so good and when it's bad it's so bad—and yet you can't seem to quit it.

Most people who dated around a bit have been in this type of situation, and when you are in it, it feels so intense and everything I say above is far from exaggeration; it is the reality of the situation. Some of us are more drawn to these particular types of relationships than others. I am one of those people who's drawn to "unavailable" men, and it's something I've given a lot of thought to, particularly because I've often been diagnosed by friends and family as not knowing what's good for me, or immature, or a glutton for punishment.

How frustrating is it when your friend is stuck in a relationship that is on-again–off-again and you find yourself in the middle of all the drama that it stirs up? It sucks, and as the friend you often want the person to just make a decision and stop talking about it. But passionate connections don't work like that; they thrive on full committal to their dysfunction. These relationships feed on parts of our emotions and psyche we sometimes don't even know are there.

I am driven by passion, so it's hard for me to ignore when I have passionate feelings for someone. I am good at convincing myself that a situation is "good enough" because, I tell myself, I don't need the kind of supportive relationships and accountability that those *other* (normal, straight) people need. This is a common phenomenon for independent- or feminist-identified women and symptomatic of the undefined in-between space we often find ourselves in. It is hard to feel safe and comfortable when the only available measures for what is safe and comfortable are normative ideas you don't abide by.

Independent women engage in passionate/dysfunctional relationships all the time, even though they seem too principled and politicized to perpetuate such problematic dynamics. As I describe in Chapter 1, we are often afraid of being cast as Desperate Girl, a role that, ironically, is based on the sexist idea that you are "needy" if you call someone you're interested in. It's really easy to internalize the fear of being needy and therefore limit how much we communicate what we want and need in our romantic relationships.

There are other conditions that facilitate passionate/dysfunctional relationships, too. As strong, independent women, we ourselves are often afraid of committing to relationships. Chasing someone who's unavailable is a really easy way to distract ourselves from the fact that we are the ones having a hard time being intimate. Also, the drama and uncertainty can be enticing and addictive. Not knowing what is going to happen or where it could go keeps you on your toes, and it also adds to the sexual tension. And who doesn't like a challenge?

Other reasons women—self-identified feminists or not—find themselves in these situations include internalized feelings that we don't deserve better, or a history of neglectful relationships. Maybe we are just experimental thrill-seekers. It's complicated to parse out what draws us to certain dynamics in relationships, but it is not uncommon to use a romantic relationship to work through things you may have experienced in the past, and sometimes a passionate/dysfunctional relationship is one of the places you feel most comfortable.

Women are often judged, generally by their friends (who, of course, know better—tsk tsk), when they're in passionate/dysfunctional relationships for not knowing what is good for them; the expectation is always that you should hold out for a more conventional relationship. It's hard to deal with the aftermath (inevitable fallouts) of these kinds of relationships, too, because you have to deal with the heavy-handed reprimands about how you should have known better, but it's more complicated than all that. Of course, we should all be seeking the healthiest of relationships, but when you shame someone for their intimate relationships, they are more reluctant to talk about it, and in some cases less likely to get the support and help they need to overcome it.

Passionate/dysfunctional relationships are not *all* bad or *all* good; they are complicated. I am more interested in validating these experiences and pushing the vocabularies we have to talk about less-than-optimal situations without shaming and blaming. It is important not to judge ourselves if we find ourselves in a passionate/dysfunctional relationship, but also to be honest with ourselves and realistic about whether these situations are serving us. These relationships happen, but how we deal with them (when we're in them and after they're over) determines how happy we are now and will be in future relationships. So it's important to pay attention to our habits when we are confronted with one. The challenge, when you're in a passionate/dysfunctional relationship, is finding the balance between being aware of what's happening and not being too hard on yourself.

Should I Drop the F-bomb?

A question that comes up regularly when talking to young self-identified feminist women is when, how, and if they should mention they are a feminist when dating someone new. My friend and fellow blogger Jill Filipovic has talked about her decision about whether to "come out" as a feminist when she's dating someone new, and how far into dating someone she should do that. Telling someone right away that you are a feminist is a good way to figure out right away if the person you're interested in is going to be intimidated, horrified, or super psyched about your feminism.

Feminist dream men are out there, we all know that, but there are lots of factors that draw us to the people we are going to date, and single-handed litmus tests never work. Many, if not most, of the guys we are going to date will not identify as feminists, but that shouldn't stop us from dating them.

Usually, when I start dating someone, I feel out the situation to see if and when it might be appropriate to drop the f-bomb. Sometimes I go for it right away (i.e., he starts the date with a conversation about how appalling the Republican cutbacks to women's health are—swoon), or sometimes I wait a little bit longer because some red flag has gone up, even though they haven't really said how they feel about it. Or sometimes all the good ideas are there, but they are not well-versed in the language of feminism per se, so it takes a little more work to connect the dots and then decide if I'm going to drop the f-bomb. Or sometimes I don't at all because they are so obviously unfeminist, but maybe I still want to sleep with them anyway. (What? I'm being honest!)

But ultimately, whether you identify as a feminist or not, you definitely don't want to be with the kind of guy who's going to be so wrapped up in antiquated ideas of what the label "feminism" means that it impacts whether he even wants to date you in the first place. And if someone I'm dating supports women's rights, the word "feminism" is not going to determine whether they want to keep dating me or not.

Many women don't identify as feminist in the first place because they are afraid it will make men not like them, and you can't blame them completely since we're taught that self-esteem is connected to male attention, and since the word "feminist" has so many negative connotations. Feminism's association with lesbianism, anger, and man-hating is a result of effective antifeminist messaging that originated to tell young women that if they identified as feminist they wouldn't get laid.

This backlash against feminism makes it more important than ever for us to confidently identify as feminists. The myth that being a feminist won't get you laid is untrue—being confident in the things you want and clear about how you are going to get them (feminist values) make you that much more attractive. Feminism makes you sexy, confident, strong, and compassionate—and why wouldn't you be excited to identify as those things?

Where Is This Going?

The question of where a relationship is going almost inevitably comes up at some point during the dating process—whether the answer is nowhere (it's over) or moving forward (toward a "real" relationship). Once you realize you like a person and they have qualities that could make for a long-term partner, you invariably start playing out scenarios in your head. Or perhaps you realize that you like the person, but since they don't have the qualities you're looking for in a long-term partner, you start trying to figure out what you want the relationship to look like.

I don't think there's anything that frustrates me more than the question, "Where is this going?" Not because I don't wonder about it myself—it is totally normal to want to know where your relationship is going—but because of all the other questions that follow: *Will my parents accept him? Does he have the kind of job that I imagined my would-be boyfriend would have? How often should we expect to see each other? Oh, only once a week, but so and so sees her boyfriend three times a week. And what does he think about marriage? Heck, what do I think about marriage? Kids? Okay, this is already going too far. I need space.* You can relate, I'm sure. When we ask where a relationship is going, we have no choice but to base it on traditional conceptions of where relationships ought to go. It is no longer defined by what is happening in the moment, but rather what you have been taught a relationship should be, which is often determined as much by external pressures as by what you need and want.

Not having a concrete goal like marriage can make figuring out the boundaries of your relationship that much more difficult since there is no standard for stability, longevity, and commitment. But the flip side of this is that it takes the pressure of the "where is this going?" question and makes it more about what two people want. You have a critical opportunity to create a relationship that is based on shared values and commitment as opposed to external forces and markers of successful romance. This requires good communication, since your relationship will be much more about personal and agreed upon goals, but is a tremendous opportunity for invention, creativity, and a type of commitment that forces you to confront the core of who you are and how you view love.

In recent years, I have been craving stability, both in my romantic endeavors and in my professional life. I have worked on delinking my self-esteem from my romantic status, but if I am not vigilant I'll fall back into the habit of conflating my success as a dater with my success as a person. I try to keep my relationships separate from my feelings around success and stability, but it's not easy to do when everyone around you is measuring their own relationships in terms of whether or not they are "going somewhere." You begin to think you have it all wrong, and that maybe you should be trying to date with an end goal in mind. But the reality is that even the most stable of committed and married relationships have moments of insecurity and instability, so finding our own sense of balance and stability outside of a romantic pairing is the best place to start.

So, I Tried an Open Relationship and ...

There are entire books written about open relationships, so I certainly can't do the topic justice in one section of a chapter. (I wholeheartedly recommend reading *The Ethical Slut*, by Dossie Easton and Catherine A. Liszt, and *Open*, by Jenny Block, two very nuanced takes on open relationships in contemporary dating.) All I can do is reflect on my observations, personal experiences, and those of my friends in open relationships.

For many, an open relationship is a concrete way to avoid and resist the pressure of heteronormativity by rejecting the monogamous structure of romantic relationships. Open relationships are sometimes the stand-in "lefty" romantic model, one that attempts to bring into question the very way that we structure desire, relationships, and families. It is important to qualify that while open relationships are a subculture movement, they span cultures and borders. Open relationships include everything from polygamy, religious-sanctioned or not, to committed relationships between three or more people, and couples who work out their own unique arrangements—and the possibilities are endless. It seems almost ridiculous to lump together everything that is not heteronormative into one category, but that is one of the side effects of having only one model that is considered legitimate.

My own experience with open relationships has not been particularly great. I tried them in two different relationships, one that started open and one that ended up open, both of which involved me having a primary partner and some basic (but frankly muddled) ground rules. I found them to be exceptionally time-consuming and emotionally draining. I am impressed with people who can curb their jealousy or feelings of guilt to the point of being able to maintain a successful primary partnership within an open relationship, but I found it to be something I couldn't maintain without quite a bit of grief and energy.

I was frustrated that an open relationship didn't work for me emotionally because I loved the idea of it theoretically and thought it could be the solution I was looking for—an intervention to heteronormativity. Part of why I had a hard time enjoying open relationships was jealousy. While I am very comfortable dating multiple people at once, I always have a favorite and I generally want to spend all my time with that person. I also don't want that person to date other people after we have gotten serious. And this particular preference of mine makes it really hard to date openly.

Another aspect of open relationships that I found hard to deal with was my perception that men are able to benefit in a way that I didn't feel like I could because of male privilege. We are socialized to believe that women can't have sex like men, and that it means something totally different for a guy to go out and have multiple sexual partners than it does for women. There's a greater social cost for women who have multiple sexual partners, making it harder to decipher what you enjoy and feel okay about it. It is also challenging to find male partners who want to be in an open relationship and who are also grounded in political ideas and don't exploit or play women.

The Ethical Slut was right to point out that open relationships are not just about "free sex" without boundaries. In fact, there is no such thing as free sex (as in, without emotion) and an effective open relationship has agreed upon rules and expectations and should be very cognizant of boundaries. Considering the social pressures you are up against, a healthy and effective open relationship is actually an act of revolution.[2]

I sometimes found that being in an open relationship pitted me against other women, something that is unacceptable for me, especially since the point of being in an open relationship was to try to apply my feminist values to my romantic life. I work hard against programming that pits women against each other (foxy lady communities unite!), so I didn't want my personal life to be a microcosm of everything that is wrong with women vying for male attention, thanks.

I found myself jealous and threatened by women I didn't even know, women I would presumably have been friends with if they hadn't been sleeping with my partner. I am very clear that jealousy between women is not just about individual and personal feelings of jealousy, but is based on a system of competition for male attention.

Open relationships work in the queer community in a different way, since the pressure of patriarchy is not the same. Two women competing for the interest of another woman has a different set of expectations on it and a completely different historical legacy. That's not to say it's not still sticky, treacherous, and challenging, but it's different. And still, regardless of gender, overcoming jealousy is no small task. I'm not saying everyone who's successful in open relationships has to be good at compartmentalizing or staying slightly detached, but in my experience these are qualities of people I know who have had successful open relationships.

One valuable lesson I learned through being in an open relationship was patience. I am not an avid anti–open relationship person just because my two experiences didn't really work for me. I say if you feel like it might work for you, then go for it. There's value in working through feelings of jealousy and being patient with yourself and your partner. And even though sometimes I was jealous, sometimes I wasn't, and that was okay. It didn't mean I liked my partner any less. It forced me to learn to be alone in my relationship, something that goes out the window when you are talking about monogamy. It also forced me to have a sense of security in myself that wasn't coming from my relationship, which was invaluable. In fact, it was this security that gave me the confidence to end the relationship and stay single until my next relationship, because I knew I would be fine on my own.

So Why Bother Dating?

Dating as a feminist combines a mixture of our politics, our emotions, what we are taught to believe about how we should love and date, and what our peers are doing. It can be challenging to navigate all of these things and come up with authentic ways to love and be with someone. As we have seen throughout this book, it's pretty much impossible for our actions, even the subversive ones, not to be impacted by the world around us and by what we have internalized about love.

It may be obvious by now that I've struggled to reconcile what I think I want and what I actually want in my romantic relationships. What I want changes depending on my mood and the person I am dating. Sometimes I am more idealistic and sometimes I am more realistic. This problem is not limited to feminists; everyone experiences it. At the core of figuring out what you need in a romantic relationship is knowing who you are and being able to connect who you are with what you need. Since my identity is wrapped up in political ideas of feminism and modern life, I am committed to a worldview that is outside of the "norm," so I end up in situations where I am figuring out what I need as I go.

Happiness itself is reliant on unrealistic standards that daters and non-daters alike are held to. But if we can rethink what we're told we need to make us happy, we can come to terms with the fact that conventional standards for dating may not make us happy. And that will open up space for us to think about what actually does make us happy—without fear of rejection, posses- siveness, or jealousy getting in the way. And that in turn gives us some space for experimentation and fun.

The fears and problems we have with dating are universal ones; everyone who wants to love and connect with someone au- thentically has to do the work of self-reflection in the face of tra- ditional and institutional expectations. From there we can start to figure out what will keep us satisfied, and then trust ourselves to make choices that align with our personal and political beliefs as well as our emotional needs. It's true, dating can really suck, but when we recognize how we are often set up to fail, we can take some of the pressure off ourselves, and the people we are dating, and just have a good time.

If you stop worrying about finding The One, you can just en- joy meeting new people and all the possible adventures that come with that. It is through the process of trial and error that we start to create the kind of relationships that do work for us. These re- lationships may never look traditional and they may not always look "feminist," but with honesty, awareness, and a solid faith in yourself, they will take on a life of their own and help you negoti- ate a new terrain for feminist love.

NAUGHTY GIRLS

NEED LOVE TOO

The erotic is a measure between the beginnings of our sense of self and the chaos of our strongest feelings. It is an internal sense of satisfaction to which, once we have experienced it, we know we can aspire. For having experienced the fullness of this depth of feeling and recognizing its power, in honor and self-respect we can require no less of ourselves.

—Audre Lorde

{ CHAPTER EIGHT } I remember all of them. Like the one I met at a party late one night who took me back to his Victorian house with stained-glass windows in the Haight district in San Francisco. We were the same height and this turned out to be a great thing. I remember fondly the grin I had on my face as I walked past all the shoppers on my way to the bus the following morning, even if I can't remember his name. Or how could I forget the one I met on the beach in Mexico? He spent his days traveling the coast of Central America playing music, making jewelry, and bodysurfing. We went back to his cabana and he had an outdoor shower. I probably don't need to say where it led from there. Then there was the one that I knew had a girlfriend. I had a boyfriend, too, but I was in an open relationship so it didn't (technically) matter. We were in our friend's apartment and it was wrong—we both knew it was wrong—but it felt so right and we did it anyway. And then we did it again.

Sex outside the parameters of a conventional relationship can be amazing. For years, the main way I expressed my sexuality was through casual sex. It made me feel powerful, independent, and in control of my romantic choices. It felt like a legitimate way to fight patriarchy and heteronormativity, one delicious experience after another. I felt pride in being able to express myself so freely and comfortably. I didn't need a boyfriend. I could have sex when I wanted and I maintained my freedom and independence.

After a couple of years, however, I began to yearn for something more, and casual sex became less "casual" than it had been for me. Encounters that had always been deeply satisfying were now making me feel destabilized, disempowered, and just downright confused. I had to face the reality that there were emotions that I had buried deep within myself about what I truly needed and wanted in my romantic life. I had to acknowledge that casual sexual relationships weren't satisfying those needs. And I had to be honest and admit that some of my feelings of empowerment were really feelings of validation coming from the attention I was getting from men for being the "sexy, cool, easy, awesome" girl.

And it wasn't just my personal feelings of needing something more that made casual sex less satisfying. I also got in tune with a larger power imbalance that existed between my ability to be casual versus that same ability on the part of the men I was sleeping with. I noticed that they were not facing similar social pressures around sexuality, shame, or inadequacy in finding love (although many of them felt it personally, just not as much from external factors). No one was telling them they should settle down because their behavior had reached an expiration date, or that if they kept it up they would never find true love. As I grew privy to this unspoken dynamic, the stakes of casual sex got much higher and my feelings around it moved from empowerment to frustration.

When we talk about casual sex we mean a sexual interaction between two consenting adults that is purely physical, with "no strings attached," no commitment of exclusivity, and no emotional attachment. Above all, no expectation of a (traditional) relationship should ever be assumed. Call it what you will—casual sex, hookups, booty calls, one-night stands, fuck buddies, friends with benefits, whatever term you've heard—they're all solid alternatives to procuring sex within the confines of a conventional romantic relationship.

But the "casual" in casual sex is in many cases a misnomer. Sex does, in fact, have emotional consequences irrespective of what kind of relationship you are having it within—just not the consequences the religious right wants to hammer us over the head with. I didn't lose self-esteem. I didn't hate my body (quite the opposite). I didn't feel like I'd diluted my sexual potency. I wasn't emotionally scarred. I wasn't diseased or suicidal. I didn't mess up my career, drop out of college, or experience any of the other consequences the anti–premarital sex crowd claims you will experience when you engage in casual or premarital sex. I simply found that casual sex does not necessarily provide an escape from patriarchy's hold over our sex lives. It wasn't the sex that was starting to feel toxic; it was the sexism. And I was frustrated with the lack of language and tools I had to address my discontentment.

Many religious and conservative groups across the country cite premarital sex (which casual sex generally is unless it's sex in the context of an extramarital affair) as contributing to the moral decline of young people. Young women, in particular, are shamed regularly for their perceived sexual promiscuity. In her book, *The Purity Myth*, Jessica Valenti writes about groups like the Concerned Women for America (CWA), who have taken on the task of upholding the "purity" of women and blaming all problems on premarital sex. Valenti writes, "It seems no consequence, from herpes to suicide, is too weighty to pin on premarital sex." (For a taste of their logic, look no further than the founder of CWA, Beverly LaHaye, who was quoted in *Woman's Touch* magazine as saying, "I believe abortion, pornography, premarital sex, and homosexuality are schemes of the devil.")[1] According to conservatives, sex outside of the confines of marriage is the end of femininity and womanhood as we know it, because what is a young woman worth to her would-be husband without her chastity, without her virginity?[2]

These archaic conservative views and definitions of sexuality have limited our ability to have healthy and holistic conversations about sex. Sex ends up being defined by what it is not—sex within a monogamous relationship, generally within the confines of marriage.

We are pigeonholed into talking about sex in extremes: either you are 100 percent okay with having casual sex or you are 100 percent onboard with waiting until marriage and saving yourself for your husband (or at the very least, in a serious relationship). This binary not only ignores how sex happens (which varies, as we all know, from awesome to regrettable), but has created a toxic climate for young women trying to figure out their own sexuality.

Casual sex is not all good or all bad. Depending on where you are in your life, what is motivating you (post-breakup trampage anyone?), and your personal history with sex, your comfort level with casual sex will differ.

The consensus about casual sex is mixed even among feminist-minded folk because of the side effects of sex in an antisex, pro-purity culture. On the one hand, we want to empower women to express themselves sexually and firmly believe in casual sex as a legitimate way to express your sexuality, fulfill your sexual desires, and experiment and learn about yourself. On the other, we want to inform and educate women about the potential pitfalls of being sexual in a culture that lacks appropriate sex education, access to contraceptives, and other reproductive health technologies.

There is a desire to protect girls and young women from sexual assault, being sexualized, early pregnancy, and other consequences of having sex. While these are legitimate concerns, insisting that abstinence is the only way to prevent them is untrue, unrealistic, and irresponsible. Pile on top of that the oversexualization of women and girls in the media, our limited resources in preventing the side effects of sex (including lack of information about STIs and access to reproductive health technologies), racist messaging around young women and sexuality, and internalized shame around sex, and we've got ourselves another feminist dating conundrum: Enjoying casual sex on your own terms in a sexist world can be challenging.

Hookup Culture and the Pleasure Principle

Teaching young women that their worth is their sexuality, whether in the deployment or denial of it, is damaging. Women who are marked "spoiled," "rotten," or "damaged" from engaging in sex are being taught that their self-worth is based on whether or not they have sex. On the other hand, when women don't "put out" they are labeled prudes, teases, bitches, or frigid. This push and pull of women's sexuality is currently creating a crisis for young women who want to express themselves sexually, but who are not finding healthy ways to do so. It is a damned if you do, damned if you don't situation.

"Hookup culture" has made a lot of news headlines in the last few years. It is basically another way to say casual sex, but it's generally referring to young people in college or high school. It is an attempt to name a particularly new development in the sexual economy where young people are sexually experimental outside of traditional courtship models.

Most talk of "hookup culture" is antisex fearmongering. According to conservatives, men have uncontrollable sexual desires that must be curbed, while women must maintain their chastity. Men are allowed to enjoy the hookup and move on while the women, who apparently don't really like sex that much in the first place, are exiled to the sad lonely village of spinsters, feminists, and whores.

As I discuss in Chapter 1, Mark Regnerus and Jeremy Uecker conclude in *Premarital Sex in America* that young women ultimately do not benefit from having sex too early. Laura Sessions Stepp concludes the same in her book, *Unhooked: How Young Women Pursue Sex, Delay Love, and Lose at Both*, which includes interviews with four cherry-picked college-aged women, all of whom prove her point that hookup culture is detrimental to women's futures. They are hitting on some real trends about young women, sex, and happiness, but, unsurprisingly, their critiques and solutions rely on unrealistic and antiquated ideas of female sexuality.[3]

There are also some thoughtful and legitimate critiques about the limits of hookup culture. Rachel J. Simmons, author of *The Curse of the Good Girl*, calls into question how effective or productive "hooking up" is for young women. She writes in her book:

> *"As a relationship advice columnist for* Teen Vogue, *I get a lot of mail from girls in 'no strings attached' relationships. The girls describe themselves as 'kind of' with a guy, 'sort of' seeing him, or 'hanging out' with him. The guy may be noncommittal, or worse, in another no-strings relationship. In the meantime, the girls have 'fallen' for him, or plead with me for advice on how to make him come around and be a real boyfriend."*

She continues:

> *"These letters worry me. They signify a growing trend in girls' sexual lives where they are giving themselves to guys on guys' terms. They hook up first and ask later. The girls are expected to 'be cool' about not formalizing the relationship. They repress their needs and feelings in order to maintain the connection. And they're letting guys call the shots about when it gets serious."*[4]

Simmons expresses legitimate concern that young women may be denying their own emotions and letting men set the rules for their relationship or non-relationship. This tendency gets intensified in the college environment where a young woman's very self-esteem is connected to "getting laid" male attention and how "cool" you can be about sex.

I would argue, however, that it's not the sex itself that is creating this dissonance between what young women want and how they feel they should act, but the different standards men and women are held to when it comes to sex.

Young male egos are stroked when they talk about the number of women they can sack and how careless and unemotional they can be about their sexual interactions. This tends to go hand-in-hand with other types of activities that college-aged people engage in, including binge drinking, drug experimentation, and lots of sex (hello, first time out of the parents' house!). Of course, not all college-aged men are sacking lots of women, or having emotionally devoid sexual encounters, but both are intimately tied to the ethos and expectation of young male identity. Youth is supposed to be your time to "fuck around."

Young women go through an experience similar to that of their male counterparts. They are experimenting with their sexuality, with drugs, with politics, with new ways of interacting with peers. The difference is that young women are instead taught by popular culture that their self-esteem is tied to male attention and having a boyfriend. Both are taught that sex is cool, but men are taught that women are disposable and women are taught that they have to hold on to that precious man.

When I talk to young feminists on college campuses they

always report how they feel like outcasts because they don't want to be part of hookup culture, or because they don't thrive on male attention and people think something is wrong with them. These women are ahead of the curve—realizing early on that there is something problematic about having your self-esteem connected to how much male attention you can get or how much sex you can have.

In the new sexual order, where casual sex and hooking up are the norm, the expectation for women is that they mirror the ethos of their male counterparts and not have emotions when it comes to sex. And in a sexual climate where you can either be "pro-sex" or "antisex," there is little room to talk about what female pleasure looks like. It is not the casual sex part that's to blame; it's the extremist attitudes that have forced young women into a place where casual sex is almost a type of rebellion. The notion that not being antisex means you're pro-sex, and being pro-sex means you're cool with "no strings attached," leads many young women to a murky place where it is very easy to privilege male desire over their own. After all, catering to male sexual desire is a much more popular and widely understood model (porn anyone?). Culturally, if we are not even talking about what a healthy female sexuality looks like (because sex is something we should be ashamed of), how can we expect young people to engage in sexual practices that prioritize female pleasure *or* emotions?

After you've been hooking up for a while, you realize that everyone has feelings when it comes to sex, and that communication, mutual respect, and having a clear understanding of the boundaries of your relationship are some concrete ways to make casual sex a pleasurable experience. One of the reasons I started to think twice about whom I was getting sexually involved with had to do with the fact that I was meeting a lot of assholes (meaning men who got their self-esteem being awful to women).

In many of these situations, I was finding that even when we wanted to have the relationship just be "casual," there was still space for them to wield male privilege over me, overcompensating for how detached they were in the encounters. Maybe they wouldn't be as nice to me in public as they could have been, or were continually flaking on plans we made. I could chalk this up to bad behavior, but it seemed like they expressed the casualness of the relationship by being mean. The fact that I was willing to be in a casual sexual relationship somehow meant I was willing to take anything.

I don't blame these scenarios on hooking up per se, but instead on a culture that exists on binaries about sex. Just as serious relationships bring certain expectations, casual sex brings with it certain assumptions about what is appropriate behavior. A mind-set based on a binary means that if women in a serious relationship require commitment and respect, women who have casual sex are always "sluts" that deserve to be dismissed and disrespected. In other words, if women wanted to be treated nicely, they would close those legs and get on the train to seriousville and be in a serious relationship.

Finally, what is often lost in conversations about hooking up is that it's supposed to be a lot of things—uncomfortable, confusing, experimental, and downright fun—for both men and women. Hooking up is not just about sexual intercourse; it is a variety of sexual experiences, most of which are pretty pleasurable. And because of this, young people are going to hook up no matter what, fearmongering notwithstanding—and that's a good thing. They will face and deal with the variety of emotions that come from hooking up, all of which help you figure out who you are and what you want in the long-term, where both sex and love are concerned.

The Not-So-Sexy Science of Slut-Shaming

Whether we're talking about hooking up or casual sex, we hold women and men to different standards, often in the name of "science." Researchers, conservative commentators, pseudoscientists, and pop psychologists have tried to prove time and time again that women can't have sex like "men," and that when they try they end up feeling shallow, empty, and dissatisfied. In Chapter 1, I talked about the faulty science that is often used to justify gender essentialist ideas of sex, but there is more.

Lately, conservatives and the media have been taken with a neurochemical called oxytocin, the supposed "cuddle" hormone. This hormone has been touted by religious fundamentalists, pop psychologists, and relationship "doctors" as the reason why women can't have casual sex. Women release oxytocin when they orgasm, which supposedly facilitates a sense of attachment. The argument goes that if you are having casual sex, because it is "no strings attached" you don't have someone to attach to (yes, it does sound like an alien tentacle, doesn't it?). The oxytocin argument has been disproved time and time again, partly because it makes a sweeping generalization based on limited scientific understanding of neurochemicals, and partly because it's an argument that's pushed by folks with other political agendas.

It goes against the very principles of science to suggest that the release of one hormone dictates an experience that is predicated on so many variables. Heather Corinna, sex-positive educator and curator of the fantastic online resource, *Scarleteen*, parsed out the science from the politics in the oxytocin debate on her blog. After looking at a number of studies, she concluded that we shouldn't make assumptions about the role that oxytocin plays in our feelings of attachment after sex. She writes, "It's often suggested that it's female orgasm that's *the* big oxytocin power surge. However, more women than men are inorgasmic, and with casual sex specifically, it's more common for women than men not to experience orgasm, especially with brand-new partners. That given, it becomes an even stranger supposition, because the roles should then be reversed, right?"[5]

The strategic use of faulty evidence about oxytocin silences how women actually feel about sex, while mischaracterizing how men feel about sex. In my experience, both men and women are emotional about sex, but they're taught to express their emotions differently, stemming from social pressures about how men and women should experience sex, which says men shouldn't get emotional and women should. Many guys will tell you that the best sex happens when they're invested in someone. And communication, as I've mentioned previously, is equally important for men as it is for women. Last I checked, knowing what is going on in your relationship instills confidence in a relationship, regardless of your gender.

I'm not going to go so far as to say that biology is not a factor in how we experience sex. I'm not a scientist. But as someone who studies the way power functions in society, and as a young person who engages in casual sexual activity, I have spent a lot of time thinking about the ways in which men and women are affected by casual sex. There's no question that the factors and circumstances of a person's life play a hugely important role in how they engage in sexual encounters—which is never taken into account in scientific studies that claim the importance of hormones like oxytocin, or that assert that men are less likely than women to bond after a sexual encounter. The reality is that we all have feelings and we all express ourselves sexually in different ways.

Researchers and scientists love to quote a 1989 study from the *Journal of Psychology and Human Sexuality* titled "Gender Differences in Receptivity to Sexual Offers," by Russell Clark and Elaine Hatfield, as evidence for why women can't have casual sex.[6] The authors studied how people reacted when a stranger walked up to them on a college campus and propositioned sex. As romantic as this sounds, perhaps unsurprisingly, all the women declined the offer and a lot of the men accepted it. But the study was flawed for a variety of reasons—the primary one being that that's not generally a scenario that leads to casual sex. Women have casual sex with men they've been hanging out with for a while, even if only for the night. Furthermore, as women we are taught that when men make random sexual advances—especially in the middle of the day—they are total creeps, so it is unlikely that women would ever respond positively to this kind of proposition. It is ultimately an issue of safety for us.

In a more recent study from the University of Michigan, Professor Terri D. Conley found that the reason women are less likely to engage in casual sex is not because they don't enjoy it, but because they feel there is a higher risk involved and a lower propensity for it to be a pleasurable experience for them.[7] In an analysis of this study, Thomas MacAulay Millar explains how this conclusion is "based as much on the social structures we participate in as men, and the ways they operate in the culture."[8] As long as we live in a culture where men are patted on the back for how much sex they have and women are shamed, where women are often blamed for rape and their victims rarely see justice, and where there is limited access to reproductive health technologies (like abortion and contraception), women will always be more hesitant to engage in casual sex than their male counterparts.

That doesn't mean women should then be blamed for these side effects of sex, but we should instead push for a culture that owns up to these realities. Unfortunately, a favorite reaction to women being at greater risk when it comes to casual sex is to suppress women's desire to have sex. Researchers, religious fundamentalists, and antisex commentators go to great lengths to show us how women can't have casual sex. Instead of seeing how women's caution and hesitance stem from social problems, we instead see women routinely shamed for having sex at all.

It is possible to have a hookup culture that includes young women's desires, emotions, and needs, but that means creating a space for it in a culture that currently privileges male desire and holds certain truths about the rightful place for female sexual expression. Until we stop relying on faulty science that suggests women don't enjoy sex and the way we respond to sex is biologically different, we will be trapped in a cycle of blaming women for their sexual choices, as opposed to focusing on larger social and structural forces that dictate sexual behavior.

Why Buy the Cow When You Can Get the Milk for Free?

Another tired argument we hear about why women shouldn't engage in casual or premarital sex is this notion that if you "give up" the sex too soon, you have nothing to hold over men's heads to keep them interested in you. "Why buy the cow when you can get the milk for free?" speaks to a commonly held belief that women's sexuality is so potent that withholding it will ensure that she's marriage material. It's equally problematic for guys, however, as it assumes that all men want is sex. It also feeds into the virgin/whore dichotomy where women's sexuality is confined to extremes. The good girl respects her body, waits to have sex, makes the man wait, and utilizes her greatest "power"—her (illusion of) chastity—in her romantic relationships. The flip side of this is a woman who doesn't know what's good for her and has too much sex, making her a whore, a spoiled woman, impure, corruptible, emotionless, unapologetic about sex, and therefore unmarryable.

Suggesting that a woman is a cow (as it were) and that her sexuality is milk that can be sold or owned is the perfect sexist metaphor. It assumes women's sexuality has transactional powers and therefore should be saved for payment after one gains male commitment. And, of course, women don't like to have sex; sex is only for the purpose of manipulating and convincing men to get married (duh). It is a sex barter system that commodifies women.

While this is an obviously problematic dichotomy, it continues to impact how women's sexual choices are made and perceived. While most progressive women don't think they are going to be virgins when they get married, it takes real work not to internalize the belief that female sexuality is a commodity and that if you give it up too soon you are ruining your chances for a long-term relationship. This is especially true when we're being force-fed the message that women's inability to keep their pants on has created a crisis in successful relationships in the first place.

Feminism takes the rap for women's willingness to "give up the milk for free," but this blame is misplaced. The mainstream media has co-opted the feminist language of empowerment, suggesting that this moment of "girl power" means that women can be super sexy and desirable to men *and* have it all. As I discuss in the introduction, the mainstream media likes to suggest that feminism's main goal is for women to act like men. (I mean what else did our feminist foremothers die for other than for our right to play "Grand Theft Auto" with as much reckless abandon as our male peers?)

This distorted view of feminism is very popular. Ariel Levy coined the term "female chauvinist pigs" in her book of the same name to describe pro-sex feminists who she believes have diluted the word "empowering" to encompass what she calls "raunch culture" and who are responsible for objectifying women. She is right that young women are heavily objectified by and in the media. But feminists are hardly the ones to blame for the overabundance of corporate-produced, pornographied caricatures of femininity. Levy's analysis falls in line with a lot of antifeminists who conflate increased sexual freedom with the objectification of women. She fails to acknowledge that (a) what she considers "feminist" in the media is a co-opted and distorted version of it, and (b) corporate enterprise and marketing have a huge impact on the production of these hypersexualized images. You cannot have a conversation about young women's sexual choices without acknowledging the real impact media depictions of women have on real girls and women.[9]

The anti–premarital sex crowd and feminists alike share the belief that these depictions have a negative impact on women's sexuality. But their solutions are diametrically opposed. The anti–premarital sex crowd believes that what's modeled in the media is to blame for throwing young women into an oversexed frenzy of orgies and blow jobs, and that feminism (or women having too much freedom) is to blame. The solution, therefore, is a call for more piety and for women to "save themselves" for marriage.

Feminists (as in real-life, actual, non-media-fantasy feminists) believe that these exploitative images in the media hurt women, too, making it difficult for us to have authentic self-images and a healthy sense of sexuality. But the solution for feminists is to continue to fight for a culture where women have control of their own sexuality and engage in healthy, confident, and self-aware sexual practices on their own terms.

Suggesting that feminism is responsible for the lack of accountability men feel in romantic relationships (because they "get the milk for free") is really effective PR to keep women from enjoying their sex lives. It keeps us shaming each other when we have sex outside of the confines of our relationships. It forces us to overcompensate for how much we enjoy casual sex. And it silently gives men an unfair advantage because they can have sex as they please and settle down whenever they're ready, and the assumption is there will be unlimited women at their disposal.

And while the virgin/whore dichotomy and the cow metaphor are not very generous in how they characterize women, they don't benefit men either. When we buy into these concepts, we see men as vagina-hungry man beasts who must be controlled through sanctions like marriage and withholding sex. But this doesn't take men's feelings into account, or the fact that men want to be in relationships, too, and if anything, the propagation of these kinds of characterizations contributes more to the masculinity crisis than women emasculating men because of their success.

Unlike women, however, men who aren't ready for relationships are accepted and considered typical and normal. People encourage men not settling down, and even condone the behavior because that is "how men are." Nothing is wrong with a man for being a bachelor, or having tons of sexual partners and not wanting to settle down.

The ways women are shamed, in the meantime, affect us in ways we don't even realize. I have several (feminist-minded) friends who think that casual hookups are all well and good, but not *after a certain age,* or *instead of a serious relationship.* These viewpoints may seem myopic, but the sentiments are more than just the internalized messaging from antisex, antiwoman advocates. Yes, there is a group of people in this country dedicated to shaming women for their sexual choices, pushing them into heteronormative relationships, shoving abstinence-only education down their throats, and basing the entire anti–premarital sex/pro-purity movement on the inability to trust women. But those are not the people I am talking about. I'm talking about women who are comfortable with casual sex culture, but who realize somewhere along the way that they want "something more."

For these women, it's challenging to have a serious relationship in part because we live in a culture that is drifting toward more casual relationships. Many women, as they get older, want to settle down and have more serious relationships because either they want to start a family or they want to be in a monogamous relationship.

The solution, however, is not to fall back on retrograde relationship models, but instead to push the parameters of how we talk about sex and relationships to include new possibilities. Part of this involves finding partners who understand this tension; part of it is knowing what you want; and part of it is undoing our own internalized beliefs around sex and love. Casual sex is not just about women making a choice to have sex when they want to. It's also about women engaging their sexuality on their own terms, and not having their experiences dictated by popular culture, by politics, or by men.

And feminism has made sex better. It's removed some of the pressure around how men and women interact and has made progress toward equalizing the power dynamics. "Sexual liberation," as it was understood in the '60s and '70s, had a profound impact on women's sexual freedom. It freed women *and* men from the belief that sex could be enjoyed only within the confines of marriage and brought sex out of the purview of male control. The fight for sexual liberation was a *good* thing because it allowed women the freedom to control what they do with their own bodies. Feminists also fought for a language of female desire, and the erotic, in efforts to separate pornographied versions of sex from more erotic models that centralized female satisfaction, communication, and experimentation. That's what feminism actually did, not what the naysayers claimed it did. I refuse to blame this movement for the current commodification of women's sexuality—that's all I'm saying.

Sexy, Slutty, and Brown

While feminism made tremendous progress in how women can express their sexuality, a lot of what's been achieved happened as a result of privilege. Today's conversation around freedom of sexual expression is very much dominated by white conceptions of sexuality. In white circles (especially liberated, feminist circles) sexuality is considered liberating and freeing, and yet, for working-class women, immigrants, and women of color it is considered (and projected onto us as) highly problematic behavior.

The mainstream media is ripe with oversexualized images of women of color, and policy often stigmatizes and shames this same group of people. Women of color and poor women are blamed for their inability to keep their legs closed and for having too many children. For marginalized groups of women, sex is not linked to pleasure or freedom; it is demonized and used as an example of all the ways in which these women lack self-control. As a result, a lot of conversations around sexual freedom discount the experience of people of color, failing to take into account how much sexual freedom is assumed to hinge on a woman's privilege—be it because of her race, economic status, or social standing.

Audre Lorde, bell hooks, Jill Nelson, Alice Walker, Leti Volpp, Saidiya Hartman, and countless other feminists of color have either directly or indirectly brought up the idea that the social consequences of sex are greater for women of color. Women are sexualized by the media, period, but women of color face a unique set of circumstances where they have historically been hypersexualized, and then held to white standards of purity. According to popular ideas of sexuality, women of color start out impure. One concrete example of this happens around rape and sexual assault. When the survivor is a woman of color, the assumption is that she started out consenting. After all, the bodies of women of color are for consumption and therefore they are always ready and willing to have sex.

Specifically, black women are often living in communities that lack access to reproductive health technologies, healthcare, and education, and have low rates of contraception use. As a result, people are quick to accuse black women of being overly sexual and unable to "control" themselves. Partially in response to this "epidemic," many religious (black and nonblack) activists have fallen in line with the antiabortion and antisex set, shaming black women for their sexual choices.

Of course, not all women of color are sexualized in the same way. For example, while black women are considered lascivious, always consenting and out of control, Latina women are considered exotic or overly sensual and Asian women are considered childish and prude. These particular stereotypes are reinforced through popular culture and pornography (just Google respectively "Asian women," "black women," or "Latina women" and then "women" and see what comes up). The common thread here is that nonwhite women's sexuality is seen as outside the norm of white heterosexuality. It's therefore something to be uniquely desired, manipulated, exploited, or controlled. Within this rather toxic climate, being a woman of color who's in touch with her sexuality is an act of resistance. Pushing past the negative media depictions and still finding a healthy, healing, erotic, and functional sexuality is no small feat.

I can't point out exactly when and where I felt uniquely sexualized as a woman of color, as opposed to just a woman—I am both at the same time. As my casual sex streak came to an end, however, I became cognizant of how my race and gender were being uniquely sexualized. There was a hidden narrative about women of color and sexuality that had been gnawing at me for years. I wasn't supposed to enjoy sex because it's not appropriate for South Asian women (we're not like those slutty American girls!). I was supposed to be ashamed and pious. It didn't matter how healthy or confident I was about my sexual choices, it still felt like I was acting in rebellion. I was not just "a sexy, cool, easy, awesome" girl but I was also a "bad Indian" girl.

I have often felt trapped between discourses of sexuality. If I'm overtly sexual, I'm a threat to what it means to be a good, pious South Asian lady *and* to white norms of sexuality. As a result, when I am sexual, I am confronting my ethnic community and the norms of white sexuality. Finding a more authentic sexuality that's just about me means pushing past what is considered the appropriate way for me to be sexual based on my race, ethnicity, and gender. This has meant a lot of experimentation, sometimes playing up how "bad" I am or being tremendously secretive about my sexual transgressions (well, clearly not after this book). And it has meant sifting through partners and figuring out which ones are a little too obsessed with my being Indian. To help you with this task, I have for you a list:

How to Know You Are Dating a Racist

1. *You realize you have never met their parents and they live down the street.* Nothing says, "I love you," like "I am embarrassed for my parents to find out you are not the race they want you to be."

2. *They love the Rolling Stones but think that Jay-Z is sexist.* I mean, I know it is hard to overlook Mick Jagger's profoundly progressive views on women, but let's just try for the sake of argument. (eyeroll)

3. *They ask you on the first date if (insert ethnicity) girls are as (insert ethnicity related explicit sexual act) as people say they are.* It's like sexist racist Mad Libs, really.

4. *They ask you offensive questions about what they perceive your culture to be, defending their profoundly ignorant question by saying, "I just want to learn more about your people, baby!"* (via @popscribblings on Twitter)

5. *They ask you if they can touch your hair or skin or eyelash or eyelid before you have even kissed.*

6. *They want to know why your family acts like "that."*

7. *They say something about how it might be easier to date someone from their own race.*

8. *When you are in a foreign country (or a taxicab), they look to you to translate even though you don't speak the language, either.*

9. *They say something to you like, "You are so different from the rest of your race. I really like you." Or, they put down other races in front of you, as though it is okay as long as they are not putting down your race.* (via Latoya Peterson)

10. *They say they noticed you because you look "exotic."* Do I look like a bird of paradise to you? (via #iamnotyourfetish)

The Feminist Art of Slutitude

It's difficult to navigate what's a healthy sexual relationship and what's an unhealthy one without some serious self-reflection and a solid analysis of gender dynamics. If you engage in healthy sexual behavior with someone who sees you as easy, is that considered healthy sex? Or, what if after having sex a few times you start to feel attached—does that mean you are less of a casual-sexer, or less of an independent, pro-sex, savvy feminist?

Look, at the end of the day, whether it's casual or not, sex is an emotional decision that requires introspection, knowing your boundaries, and a lot of experimentation. Do you have to be on top of all of this to have good sex? No. But it helps to be thinking about it (and it sometimes helps to be on top, too). Sex isn't just one static "thing" that you just "do." It's not just one act. It's a series of events that build up based on communication, cues, and sensitivities. Sex can be a variety of things, and suggesting that it's only penetration for the sake of getting off ignores that it's part of a larger process that involves intimacy and expressing yourself and your desires.

It's hard to have a frank discussion about wanting to have sex when there is so much judgment around women's sexuality, but sex is something intimate you share with someone, and you should always feel good about it. If you are having a lot of casual sex and you start to feel like it's not that casual and you have emotions involved, that doesn't mean the casual sex part is bad. It might mean that you need to start finding ways to talk with your sexual partners about what you're feeling. What makes us feel bad is how we're taught to believe that we have to be either/or in our romantic endeavors (100 percent casual or 100 percent serious). But it's completely okay to date someone casually for a long time, or to express feelings to someone you are just casual with. If they can't handle it, they may not be cut out for your sophisticated take on relationship matters!

Being accountable and being committed are two different things, and it is perfectly fine to ask a casual sex partner to be accountable. I've had my feelings hurt by people I've engaged in casual sex with. When, for instance, a guy I was dating made plans with me and then didn't show up, or when another guy said he wanted to see me again and then never called, I felt unimportant and unworthy, and like I didn't have the right to be upset because it was just casual. And yet, I felt disrespected, and it wasn't because I wasn't honest or comfortable with having casual sex, but because the other person was in fact being disrespectful in an attempt to show just how casual the situation really was. These kinds of consequences are part of the virgin/whore complex as well. Men have internalized the belief that women who "sleep around" are not to be respected, even if inside they may feel like they should be respecting them. But just because a relationship is casual doesn't mean it has to be disrespectful.

Embracing casual sex as a legitimate option means navigating the complex messages we receive about our sexuality and finding a space to authentically express and seek the pleasure we want. We can't be ashamed of our desire. Not all of us are in monogamous relationships. Many of us want to have casual sex, period, and we have every right to go out and get it. Feminist sexpert Jaclyn Friedman calls this embracing "slutitude." She wrote in a guest post for *Feministe,* "[S]luthood keeps me centered. It keeps me from confusing desire and affection with something deeper. It means I have another choice besides celibacy and settling. It means I won't enter another committed relationship just to satisfy my basic need for sex and affection. It gives me more choices, it makes room for relationships to evolve organically, to take the shape they will before anyone defines them."[10]

Fear around slutiness borders on the belief that women having sex for pleasure will no longer need traditional relationships because they're getting satisfaction outside of committed relationships. And the fear is valid! Women don't need to be in traditional or heteronormative relationships to get their kicks—and that's a good thing. It gives us the space to experiment, to feel less pressure to find The One, and it allows us to make better and more informed decisions about the people we ultimately want to be with.

The way casual sex has changed the romantic landscape for young women is a good thing, even if at first it looks scary or uncertain. Amanda Marcotte writes at *Pandagon* that these tensions diminish as girls get older and get their self-esteem from sources other than male validation, "and once the dynamic starts to shift, it creates a feedback loop. As both men and women get better at internally directed self-esteem, they become legitimately more attractive, and real love between partners becomes more of a possibility."[11]

But as Marcotte and many of us lament, the fact that it does *eventually* get better doesn't change how much power young men have in validating young women. The tension between old and new forms of dating is creating the space for experimentation, but it can also bog us down when it feels like it isn't going anywhere. Giving young women the tools and space to feel creative about expressing their sexuality and allowing them the space to experiment will make them healthier, more confident partners in the long run. Relegating young women to traditional forms of dating only pushes them further back to repressing their feelings, reinforcing false ideas of what "romance" is. A woman's power does not arise from her denial of pleasure to herself and her potential partner, but her educated, happy, successful exploration and expression of it. That is what self-empowered sexuality looks like.

I have no regrets about my adventures in casual sex, but I learned a lot along the way. Today I know that I am the sexy, cool, easy, awesome girl, not just because I am able to bed a man or because I am able to get male attention, but because my identity is not dependent on whether I am sexually active or not. I have done the hard work on myself in other parts of my life that have nothing to do with sex, and I've learned how to define and express myself in areas of my life that are not directly connected to my sexuality. My independence and knowledge of random genres of music, clothing, books, food, and travel make me who I am. My deep lasting relationships with other people make me sexy, and it's feminism that's given me the tools to express this sexiness without fear or shame.

THE ART OF
FEMINIST
Romantic Maintenance

It is against such sorrow, such spiritual death, such deliberate strangulation of the lives of women, my sisters, and of powerless peoples—men and women—everywhere, that I work and live, now, as a feminist, trusting that I will learn to love myself well enough to love you (whoever you are), well enough so that you will love me well enough so that we will know, exactly, where is love: that it is here, between us, growing stronger and growing stronger.

—June Jordan

{ CHAPTER NINE } If the last eight chapters have shown us anything, it's that feminism and dating are constantly pitted against each other. Story after story has decried that female independence and earning power have ruined romance as we know it, chivalry is dead, and, as punishment for our sins, we are going to die alone. Conventional relationships are too limiting, and the alternatives are problematic at best: men are no longer "men" and most of us can't even afford love anymore.

Finding hope in our romantic efforts can start to feel defeating, but there is some hope. It lies not only with our ability to sort out the messages we're getting about how we're supposed to love, but also with how we apply our worldviews to our behaviors. We have the power to redefine our relationships. From mainstream conversations about gay marriage, to the decline in marriage as the norm, to redefining for ourselves what our relationships look like, we have an opportunity to do our relationships differently. And feminism is here to help us.

Feminism is considered "icky," and a major reason young women don't like to identify as feminist is because they are afraid that they will be judged, they won't get married, and the boys will not be attracted to them. The antifeminism PR campaign that equated feminism with man-hating and lesbianism was very effective in convincing people that being a feminist is an unattractive choice that will never get you laid.

But we have to move past these negative stereotypes of what it means to be a feminist, because (a) they are false generalizations that don't accurately describe feminist women, who are in fact a complicated and diverse bunch, and (b) they are sexist stereotypes used to keep us complacent in a narrative that demands we are shaky, uncertain about what we want, and at the mercy of male attention.

The reality is that feminism, independence, and empowerment can only help our romantic relationships, but it requires awareness and persistence. Feminist dating requires maintenance and continually grounding yourself in what you believe in to inform you as you carve out the types of relationships that satisfy you. As with any type of social activism, patience and perseverance will lead to positive outcomes—you just have to hang in there.

This chapter is a reflection on some of the important ways feminism can help us in our dating situations, including some advice from some of your favorite feminists, all of whom I asked the same question: How does feminism make your love life better?

Feminism helps you figure out exactly what you want.

With all the messaging in the mainstream media about how women should act when it comes to dating, it can be hard to figure out what you want for yourself, what you should want for yourself, and what the world around you wants. As women, we are taught that our very existence—the way we look, talk, think, and act—has to be connected to the men we attract. We're expected to base our identity on the success of our relationships. But this doesn't have to be true. Feminism helps you separate out the fantasy of what women should want and what women should be from the actual reality of what we want and who we are. Being confident in who you are, regardless of what the mainstream media tells you, helps you decipher exactly what you want, not only out of your romantic relationships, but also in your overall life.

For years, I dated for the sake of dating, because my self-esteem was caught up in what my romantic partners thought of me and whether or not I was in a relationship. It took me a while to figure this out, but most people are insecure about dating. It was such a relief to realize this, and to be able to actively see myself as more than something that was for the purpose of male consumption. Part of being able to see this had to do with getting older and becoming more confident in who I was, but another big part of it had to do with unlearning the damage that mainstream media depictions of women and romance had done to my sense of self. Once I was able to remove myself from that line of fire, I finally started meeting people who respected me for who I was, not for who I thought I should be.

One of the most feminist things you can do is define what you want in your romantic relationships and ask for it. We have to set the standards and expectations we want from our romantic relationships and then seek partners who can meet us there. That doesn't mean dating doesn't still have its challenges, but knowing what you want out of your dating situations and being clear about those expectations is invaluable. It forces you to be accountable to yourself and will help you weed out partners who are not good for you.

Twanna A. Hines: *Women wage different self-esteem battles than men do. For much of my twenties—and, especially, my teens—I didn't like myself. I thought there was something wrong with me. I worried everyone else somehow had a special "secret" to navigating life that somehow wasn't passed along to me. In love, that meant I occasionally dated men who didn't value me as much as they should. How could they? They were merely reflecting the self-worth I projected. Becoming a better feminist means understanding I am worth more than I sometimes credit myself. I deserve* *men who love me. Each time I make an effort to understand my body better and show men how to please me, I'm doing myself a service. That's what the feminist movement teaches me.*

—Twanna Hines is a New York City–based sex
writer and runs the blog *Funkybrownchick.com.*

Jennifer Pozner: *But maybe the most incredible thing feminism has done for my love life is this: it has allowed me to understand that I am not a failure if I do not have a perfect, committed romantic relationship—or any relationship at all. Feminism has given me an antidote to all those insipid rom-coms, every scare-tactic glossy* Glamour *or* Cosmo *headline, that insist that women are pathetic, desperate losers who can never be happy without an engagement ring from some guy—any guy, even a verbally or physically abusive guy. Instead, feminism has taught me that it is absolutely ok to want love—to crave it, even—but that love can only flourish where there is mutual respect, intelligence and passion.*

—Media critic Jennifer L. Pozner is founder and
Executive Director of Women In Media & News,
and author of *Reality Bites Back: The Troubling
Truth about Guilty Pleasure TV.*

Feminism is sexy.

Feminism taught me how to love my body and therefore how to have better sex. Images of women in the media are often oversexualized, exploitative, or simply images we can't relate to. It's pretty much impossible not to internalize the belief that to feel and look sexy you have to look like what you see in the media. Recognizing the impact that kind of messaging has on how you see yourself is the first step to undoing the damage being done to us. Loving your body, despite negative programming, is an act of resistance, and will lead you to be more confident. It gives you permission to be more comfortable with what you look like, how you feel in your skin, and what your body is capable of. Loving your body and being confident lead to giving off a sexier attitude and therefore attracting more people—and to having better sex. Confidence is the best aphrodisiac.

It's true that sexual liberation was and is a great thing. But were the sexual politics of the '70s as problematic as they were liberating? You bet. And yet, one thing was made clear: women should be able to control their own sexuality. However, between regressive legislation that is cutting back on funding for reproductive health to the mass glorification of objectified and overly sexualized images of women in the media, women can't and don't get to control our own sexuality. How we feel, what we want, and what we need are rarely a primary concern in the public arena.

Feminism helps you decipher what is shitty messaging and what is real. Feminism makes it clear that being objectified is problematic, and so is the state barring our access to the means we need to control our bodies. We get to control when we want to have sex and when we don't. If you want to have sex, have sex. If you don't want to have sex, don't have sex. When you begin to free yourself from the belief that you have to be in a heteronormative relationship to enjoy sex, you begin to enjoy sex in new and different ways. When you decide that you want to be in a relationship, you can be empowered in that decision. If you are a woman who dates men, are there still going to be power differentials? Yes. If you are anybody who dates anyone, are you still going to meet assholes? Yes. But understanding feminism helps you understand the power politics that exist between you and your lover both inside and outside the bedroom—and that will lead to more effective communication, the ability to stand up for yourself, and ultimately more satisfying relationships.

Feminists have better sex because we know how to enjoy ourselves. As Jessica Valenti writes in *Full Frontal Feminism*, "There is nothing more hackneyed than the notion that feminists hate sex (but I guess if you buy the ugly, man-hating stereotype, hating sex follows). Feminists do it better 'cause we know how to get past all the bullshit."[1] We know that male pleasure is not the purpose of sex (even though that can be an exciting part of it), so we prioritize—and nothing is more attractive than that.

Rebekah Spicuglia: *Feminism helped me love myself, to value my individuality as well as my connection to the community of women and men who place importance on the human rights of women. Which include a fundamental respect for the choices we make and appreciating who we are outside of social expectations and restraints. As a noncustodial mom, this is so important to me, and as a woman over 30 with a body that has changed and a mind that requires intellectual stimulation, it's been so satisfying sexually and every other way to know what works for me and what doesn't. Sticking to it is always a challenge! But I'm so self-aware now, and that is sexy.*

—Rebekah Spicuglia is an advocate for noncustodial parents and a media strategy and communications consultant.

Feminism helps you get in *touch* with yourself.

That's right, getting in touch with yourself will make you feel better about your dating and sex life. Feeling down and out about that date that didn't go right? Go home and get in touch with that rabbit, your finger, your dildo, whatever it is you need to get yourself to that orgasmic place. I have always said that it's much less drama and much more satisfying to go home and get myself off than to have bad sex with someone I don't want in my house. Don't compromise what's important to you for fear of being alone. And don't listen to what the fundies tell you: masturbation and orgasms are good for you, your soul, your self-esteem, and your sleep cycle. It's been scientifically proven.

Lori Adelman: *Being a feminist made my love life better because it has helped me come into my own and be more confident and engaged, which in turn helped me to attract stronger, more thoughtful, and more civically engaged partners. It has enriched my sex life by making me more communicative, and self-sufficient in seeking pleasure. It makes for a good dinner conversation or opening line. And perhaps best of all, my feminist title places me in the company of a dynamic community of brilliant, sexy, fierce, and conscious people—and potential partners.*

—Lori Adelman is a Brooklyn-based writer, blogger, and advocate for women's health and rights both domestically and internationally.

Vanessa Valenti: *First and foremost, being a feminist in love allows for better sex. There ain't no other way to say it. It also allows me to live with someone, but not for them. It allows me to express* *my needs and desires without feeling like a nag or any other fe-male-in-relationship stereotypes you can think of. It allows me to love and be loved without reservations, but leaves room to maintain love for myself.*

—Vanessa Valenti is the cofounder of *Feministing.com* and online strategist living in New York.

Feminism gives you the courage to walk away when a situation is not meeting your needs.

Most of us have stayed in a relationship that is not meeting our needs because of fear of being alone. Sometimes we even stay in situations that are bad for us. Fear of being alone often comes from being socialized to believe your self-worth is based on your relationship status. The internalized belief that women must always be in relationships has devastating consequences. It is responsible for cycles of violence in relationships, for women staying in situations that are not good for them, and for settling for partners who don't make us happy.

Yes, being single can be a scary prospect considering how single women are treated, but don't let the negative talk get you down. Being single is a tremendous opportunity to think about what you want. It's a chance to focus on yourself and your own dreams, an opportunity to think about what makes you happy in your own life. It also gives you time to bond with friends and build new types of communities that don't focus on dating and couples.

Breaking up with someone who isn't meeting your needs is empowering. You get to start over—to travel, write, read, eat great food, build on new and existing friendships, and bask in the glory of being you. It's a time of no compromises. And leaving someone who wasn't good or right for you actually ensures that you'll be that much more satisfied in your future relationships—because there's nothing more empowering than going after what you know is right for you, even when there's not someone waiting in the wings to break your fall. In fact, *especially* when there's no one in the wings. I know this is all easier said than done, but having the strength to stand on your own in a world that celebrates coupledom ensures you have the tools to be empowered and happy throughout your life, both romantically and otherwise.

Lisa Jervis: *Being a feminist has helped me clarify what I want from my partnership and what's good for me to have outside of partnership. It has helped me understand the cultural landscape of dating and thus protected me from taking the sexism in that landscape personally. It's helped me understand and assert my own queer identity in the context of a life that to the casual/unobservant observer might look like that of a gender-normative straight girl. It's made me more confident in asking for what I want in bed. It's brought a community that can offer solace in the face of heartbreak. It's helped me avoid dating douchebags!*

—Lisa Jervis is the founding editor and publisher
of *Bitch* magazine and a nonprofit technology strategist.

Katie Halper: *When it comes to dating, I need to keep a feminist eye on my more insecure self. For reasons I don't have the time, paper, and toner to get into, I tolerate things from men that I shouldn't and wouldn't in people I'm not romantically interested* *or involved in. I shudder when I remember things that guys I've dated have said that I ignored or justified by telling myself "he doesn't really mean that." But it's during these moments that my feminism saves me from myself. Of course, I shouldn't be considering dudes like this in the first place, but were it not for feminism and that voice that says "exploitative relationships and gender dynamics that your great-great grandmother fought against under the Tzar, aren't cool," who knows where I'd be. So thank feminism, not God, I'm single and not married to a man I'd spend half my time helping network and the other half feeding.*

—Katie Halper is a progressive comedian, filmmaker, blogger, history teacher, and native New Yorker.

Feminism helps you not judge yourself when a situation is not working out.

Part of figuring out what you want is making mistakes. Sometimes, as strong assertive women, we are extra hard on ourselves when we don't act the way we think we should act in our dating lives. This hurts us, too. Sometimes it's okay to do what feels right in the moment, even if it doesn't make sense in the grand scheme of things. My number one rule is if it makes you happy, go for it. We can debate what happiness means, and whether you are really happy, or whether your happiness hinges on living up to someone else's expectations of happiness, but feminism helps you figure out that part, too.

Doing what feels right for you in any given moment, irrelevant of what others say, is important in helping you figure out what you want out of your romantic relationships. Check in with yourself and be honest. Are you getting what you need and want out of a situation? Are you feeling happy most of the time? Or are you stressed out, obsessed, and disappointed?

As friends to one another, we need to judge other women less and listen to them when they are figuring out the complexities of their romantic choices. Judgment just leads to our not feeling like we can share with our friends what we are going through. Inadvertently, we uphold standards that use "normal" relationships as the model through which we determine whether or not our behavior, or our friends' behavior, is appropriate or not. Expecting your friends to give ultimatums to the people they're dating in the service of holding out for a more traditional relationship is unfair; you don't want that done to you, so don't do it to others, and if your friends put you in that position, call them out on it.

Having the courage to make mistakes and not judge yourself for them is at the heart of a feminist view of love. We are all doing the best we can with the tools that have been given to us, negotiating our feelings and our deeply personal histories and beliefs. Sometimes that leads us to some uncomfortable places, but we have to be gentle with ourselves as we figure out how to navigate this new terrain of redefining how we see, practice, and understand romance.

Jaclyn Friedman: Feminism has taught me that I can define love and sex on my own terms, and seek out people who are compatible with what I want. It's shown me that I have the right to hold out for sex that's pleasurable, and love that makes myself and my partner stronger together than we would be apart. Feminism has also made me a happier, more grounded person in general, and that makes me a whole lot more fun to be with!

—Jaclyn Friedman is a feminist sexpert, editor of
Yes Means Yes: Visions of Female Sexual Power and a World Without Rape, and author of *What You Really Really Want: The Smart Girl's Shame-Free Guide to Sex and Safety.*

Feminism is all about building a solid group of friends.

So, you've tried everything and ultimately you are still coming up short in your romantic endeavors. You've had your heart broken again, you feel lonely, you feel like you are going to be single and die alone. These feelings are normal, but the best way to feel less alone is by building a strong community of friends that helps you feel less alone. Isolating yourself only makes it worse, but having people around you that make you feel good about yourself takes pressure off feeling like you have to be in a relationship. Feminism is all about community, and if that community is a book group or a group of gals to hit the town with, then that's great either way. This world is hard enough. Don't go it alone. It is so much better with friends who can support you, give you advice, and feel your pain.

The problem with our culture being so couple-centric is that when you are not in a couple, every institution is built to make you feel like there is something wrong with you. We have lost the community aspect of life in favor of a much more individualized way of living. In other countries, when families live together, they often have rich support networks that enhance and support them. We don't live in a culture that is structured in this way, but that doesn't mean we can't create the communities we need and want. In fact, doing so is an act of revolution. Forget couples-only events and let Valentine's Day be a group party whether you are in a relationship or not. Let's expand our definition of relationships to include our friends and other associates. Single people can't do it alone; we need the help of our coupled friends to help support this new romantic world order.

Ann Friedman: *Simple, really: Feminism is how I know I'm not crazy and alone.*

—Ann Friedman is the executive editor of
GOOD magazine and a former editor at *Feministing.com*.

Feminism reminds you to put yourself first.

When you are dating or interested in someone, it is easy to get caught up in that person and forget about yourself. This is the tipping point, where you can start to use their actions as a guide for your own happiness and success. This is a difficult but common cycle to get caught up in, and all the more reason to get to know and love yourself as a single person before you get into a relationship. This way you don't ever lose your sense of self when you are dating someone.

Women are taught to put others first—to nurture, mother, and sister all the men in our life. Frankly, these roles are fulfilling, but it is important to also prioritize yourself. Feminism sheds light on the social pressure women feel to serve and to nurture. Of course, it is important to be compassionate and to take care of people, but don't do it at the cost of your own happiness. Sacrificing your happiness won't benefit anyone and will only hurt you and the long-term happiness of your relationship.

Amanda Marcotte: *Getting the right relationship starts with being happy being single. This gives you leverage. It means you can hold out for a guy that makes you happy, and it means that guys you date can't walk all over you because they believe that you need them to "save" you from singlehood. A man who believes you can walk out the door and be perfectly fine on your own is a man who will think twice before cheating on you or treating you like shit. Being actually able to do it means you'll be happier, because sleeping alone is always preferable to sleeping next to someone you resent or even hate.*

—Amanda Marcotte is a freelance writer and blogger who writes regularly for *Pandagon*, *Double X*, and *RH Reality Check*.

Nona Willis Aronowitz: *Feminism is responsible for my healthiest, longest-term relationship to date. Feminism allows me to think of relationships in terms of personality traits rather than "roles." I hate doing the dishes, but it's not because I'm more masculine. It's because I fucking hate doing the dishes!*

—Nona Willis Aronowitz is a twenty-six-year-old multimedia journalist from New York City and author of *Girldrive: Criss-Crossing America, Redefining Feminism*.

Jamia Wilson: *Feminism has made my love life better because it has strengthened my understanding of the importance of loving and respecting myself in relation to how I interact with others.*

—Jamia Wilson is Vice President of Programs at the Women's Media Center where she works on amplifying women's voices and changing the conversation in the media.

Feminism makes for more equal partnerships.

Everything we are taught about relationships is gendered. From the modeling we get in society about men's roles versus women's, to the way relationships are portrayed on TV and in the movies, gender difference is alive and thriving. What we are taught about being a "man" and being a "woman" is directly connected to how we believe we are supposed to act in our relationships. And undoing this is not easy. Even when we say we are not going to manifest unequal gender dynamics, it's hard to stay honest to that intention because everything about how we are taught to interact is gendered.

And sometimes we may not want to be 100 percent equal in the sense that there might be things that a woman is traditionally expected to do and she might also like it (i.e., a woman who is expected to do the cooking and the cleaning but won't have it any other way). But being equal partners is not about actually splitting up the housework evenly, or even about who pays more; it's about separating those acts from what is expected of you based on your gender. And that means being cognizant of when we hold men to unfair expectations of what we expect of them based on their gender as well.

A lot of times the role we play in a given relationship is just about common sense: who has more money, who has more free time, who likes to cook more, who likes to clean more. These divisions themselves, of course, are often gendered due to the structural nature of gender difference (i.e., men might make more money because statistically men make more money, while women are expected to clean and therefore clean more often without even realizing it). Understanding that these divisions are gendered, however, is half the battle. Feminism helps you navigate all the nuanced ways that gender plays out behind closed doors in your relationships. There is no one way to have a feminist and equal relationship; it takes being aware of power dynamics and expectations and addressing them as they come up.

Janna Zinzi: It's been a wake-up call about how I've bought into stereotypes and expectations that are unrealistic and unfair to women. I'm still untangling that web because these stereotypes are relentlessly marketed and reinforced to girls and women (media, movies, books, articles, friends & family, etc.) and sometimes we don't even realize how we are living out these stereotypes. Feminism opens the door to breaking down these expectations and giving both men and women freedom in relationships to be who they are and to live and act in ways that feel right to them.

—Janna Zinzi is a social media consultant and owner
of Swirl Public Relations, cofounder of the *Goddesses Rising* blog,
reproductive justice advocate, and burlesque dancer.

Latoya Peterson: It's kind of hard to put into words, but the best thing about loving while feminist is the freedom involved with it. It's a little scary at first—if you drop all the pretenses spoon-fed by dating gurus and Cosmopolitan, there is a lot of emptiness there. It's acknowledging that your partner is a flawed human being, not some decoder ring you pull out of a cereal box. It's about acknowledging that you are also a flawed human being, and figuring out who you are—because if you don't know who you are, how will you find a partner that complements you? But then, into that vast silent vacuum comes clarity. You worry less about being the right size or having the right make-up technique or saying the right things or going to the right clubs, and more about what you admire in yourself and what you admire in others. It's gaining the confidence to look at what society is selling and to say, simply, "This isn't my style." It's not being frustrated about your partner not living up to someone else's idea of what a perfect match is. It's about defining your own timeline, based on what makes sense for your life. It's about acknowledging that sometimes people are single, and your life isn't terrible because you aren't partnered. And it's about having the confidence to blaze your own trail with your partner—society be damned.

—Latoya Peterson is a hip-hop feminist and editor
of *Racialicious* who has been happily dating another
hip-hop nerd with feminist tendencies since 2006.

Feminism reminds you that it's okay if it doesn't last forever.

Feminism helps push you past your comfort level when you are thinking about the limits of a relationship. It gives you the tools to realize that often "forever" is not a reality, but a corporate-produced, religiously sanctioned necessity that is not actually based on how humans behave. Yes, of course people can settle down and couple for their whole lives, and more power to them. But you can't put that kind of pressure on every single relationship you are in. It is a recipe for disaster and blinds you to certain potentially problematic dynamics in your relationship in the name of *forever.* Learning to roll with the punches and truly enjoy the time you have with the people you are dating not only helps make your current relationship stronger, but makes you stronger if something happens and you are no longer with that person.

People like to cite divorce statistics as though they're a sign that society as we know it is falling apart. The opposite is actually true. Perhaps the institution of marriage is falling apart, but high divorce statistics tell us that people are working to figure out what they want in their romantic lives in larger numbers than ever before. It is easy to get caught up in the hysteria of what high divorce rates mean, but the reality is that an unhappy and unhealthy marriage is much worse for society and for an individual's health than high divorce rates. Maybe if there weren't such pressure to get married, fewer people would leap to do so. Not to mention that there are plenty of people who end their marriages on very cordial and even friendly notes—simply realizing that ending the union is better for both parties and moving about their lives better for having had the relationship, but also realizing that it wasn't supposed to last forever.

Longevity is not the only litmus test for a successful relationship, after all. Figuring out what you want and getting those needs met is a much better indicator of a successful relationship, regardless of whether it lasts one year or fifty years. Learning to relax and roll with the punches is something feminism can help you do, because as long as you are happy with yourself, you are never alone. Finally, if what you really crave is forever, it might be good to think about why you feel that way. Most of you will discover that it's either social pressure or fear of dying alone. The first controls you, and the other is something you have no control over. As I said above, understanding why we operate the way we do is half the battle. Being armed with knowledge helps us move forward and be more present to the relationships we have, making us value them for what they have to offer us today and not cling to the ways they are supposed to serve us in the future.

Deanna Zandt: Feminism has taught me the value of myself. It's taught me that being alone is fine (and even downright good) when there aren't any strong romantic prospects; on the other end of the spectrum, it's also taught me that vulnerability, when both partners treat it with deep respect and love, makes the bond with a lover stronger through the emotional intimacy it creates.

—Deanna Zandt is a media technologist and the author of Share This! How You Will Change the World with Social Networking.

Feminism reminds you that love, just like feminism, is for everyone.

When you are in the moment, heartbroken, frustrated, or just in a relationship that is not meeting your needs, it is easy to forget that you know what's best for you. Many of us act from the heart rather than from the head when we find ourselves in these kinds of situations. The only reason I know this to be true is because I've done it—lots of times.

This is where finding a way to make feminism work for me changed the way I look at love. Feminism is the reason I'm more conscious of my behavior, as opposed to being in the doldrums of convention, continually unhappy, continually hitting walls. It allowed me the space to feel good about myself, even though society told me I was a failure for not being "successful" at finding love. Feminism moved me from desperation to hope, because I realized I wasn't alone.

For me, feminism meant building healthy communities with other people who love and understand me, communities that had nothing to do with whether I was dating someone. And it meant redefining happiness outside of what society expected of me and not using generic markers of "happiness" (i.e., in love, married, baby on the way) to gauge my own happiness. It meant pushing back on my parents and the South Asian community I'm a part of when I felt too much pressure to get married. And it meant and continues to mean asking for the things I need and want from the people I'm dating (this was by far the hardest for me). And it is about continually checking in with myself when a situation is not meeting my needs and being honest with myself about why.

I know what it feels like to feel like you need to find a relationship and that your time is running out. But buying into this type of fear won't actually lead you to happier romantic relationships. What leads to happier relationships is being empowered, honest, intentional, and clear about what you want. Feminism is constructed in the mainstream as a boner-killer, which has been very effective in keeping young women disinterested in it, but prioritizing your own needs in your romantic life is one of the primary messages of feminist dating, and the truth is we have too much to lose going about it any other way.

If each one of us commits to finding love on our own terms and maintaining a more radical love that recognizes community, global compassion, and authenticity, it will resonate throughout our communities. In a 2007 *AlterNet* article, my good friend and colleague Courtney Martin wrote, "Who you love and how you love them is as much a statement about your social con-science—perhaps even a far more accurate and moving state-ment—as the letters you write to Congress or the votes you cast. It is harder to be good to someone else. It has the potential to make them be good to others. And others are the fulcrum of social change."[2] Other people will take our lead and push against undue pressure to date, love, and marry in a specific way. A radi-cal imperative for love is possible now more than ever before, but we have to stay positive, committed, and intentional. And we have to believe that our acts of self-love and radically loving oth-ers will echo far and wide—even ultimately to groups of people who never thought loving could be outside of the conventions we have drilled into our psyches.

Love is one of the most fundamental and effective tools each of us has, and as individuals and collectively we need to use it to come together in ways beyond simply coupling. We need to use it to come together in community. As our lives become increasingly isolated, loving is one of the most radical ways to resist oppres-sive conditions, to express our love without limits, and to push for the kinds of romantic communities we want. Resisting romantic expectations, redefining romance for ourselves, and creating the kinds of relationships that will be truly satisfying are not just acts of self-love, but radical acts of feminist love that will resonate far beyond just our own relationships, but to the greater world around us.

NOTES

{ CHAPTER ONE }

Feminism Didn't Ruin Dating, Dating Ruined Dating

1. Sozio, Donna and Samantha Brett. *The Man Whisperer: A Gentle, Results-Oriented Approach to Communication* (Avon, MA: Adams Media, 2011), p 33.
2. Springer. "Feminism and Romance Go Hand in Hand." *ScienceDaily*, October 16, 2007.
3. Rudman, Laurie A. and Julie E. Phelan. "The Interpersonal Power of Feminism: Is Feminism Good for Romantic Relationships?" *Sex Roles* 57, October 6, 2007, 787–799.
4. Stork, Travis L. *Don't Be That Girl* (New York, NY: Simon Spotlight Entertainment, 2008).
5. U.S. Census Bureau, 2005.
6. www.unmarried.org, www.census.gov/acs/www.
7. "Women in America: Indicators of Social and Economic Well-Being." March 2011: www.whitehouse.gov/sites/default/files/rss_viewer/Women_in_America.pdf.
8. Barnett, Rosalind and Caryl Rivers. *Same Difference* (Cambridge, MA: Basic Books, 2005), 85–86.

9. Fine, Cordelia. *Delusions of Gender: How Our Minds, Society, and Neurosexism Create Difference* (New York, NY: W. W. Norton and Co., 2010), 5.

10. Fisher, Helen. *Why We Love* (New York, NY: Henry Holt and Co., LLC, 2004), 51–55.

11. Knox, Richard. "Study: Men Talk Just as Much as Women." *NPR*, July 5, 2007: www.npr.org/templates/story/story.php?storyId=12633456

12. Fine, 151.

13. Regnerus, Mark. "The Case for Early Marriage." *Christianity Today*, July 31, 2009: www.christianitytoday.com/ct/2009/august/16.22.html.

14. Regnerus, Mark and Jeremy Uecker. *Premarital Sex in America: How Young Americans Meet, Mate, and Think about Marrying* (New York, NY: Oxford University Press, 2011).

15. Serano, Julia. *Whipping Girl* (Berkeley, CA: Seal Press, 2007), 19.

{ CHAPTER TWO }

Searching for Citizenship in the State of Love

1. Friedman, Ann. "On the Outs." *The American Prospect,* April 16, 2010: www.prospect.org/cs/articles?article=on_the_outs.

2. Perez, Miriam. "Al and Tipper Gore to Separate after Forty Years of Marriage." *Feministing.* June 2, 2010: http://feministing.com/2010/06/02/al-and-tipper-gore-to-separate-after-forty-years-of-marriage.

3. Traister, Rebecca. *Big Girls Don't Cry* (New York, NY: Free Press, 2010).

4. Wise, Tim. "This is Your Nation on White Privilege," *Red Room,* September 13, 2008: www.redroom.com/blog/tim-wise/this-your-nation-white-privilege-updated.

5. Sarkar, Tanika. *Hindu Wife, Hindu Nation* (Bloomington, IN: Indiana University Press, 2001), 3.

6. Rowland, Debran. *Boundaries of Her Body: A Troubling History of Women's Rights in America* (Naperville, IL: Sphinx Publishing, 2004), 83–85.

7. Honey, Maureen. "The Working-Class Woman and Recruitment Propaganda during World War II: Class Differences in the Portrayal of War Work. *Signs,* 8:4 (Summer 1983), 672–687.

8. Harris-Perry, Melissa. "The War on Women's Futures." *The Nation,* March 3, 2011.

9. Centers for Disease Control. "Cohabitation, Marriage, Divorce, and Re-marriage in the United States." July 2002.

10. Centers for Disease Control. "Births, Marriages, Divorces, and Deaths: Provisional Data for 2009", table A, 2010.

11. Smith Foster, Frances. *'Til Death or Distance Do Us Part: Marriage and the Making of African America* (New York, NY: Oxford University Press, 2010).

12. Harris-Lacewell, Melissa. "Rethinking Marriage: The World Has Changed. It's Time." *AlterNet*, October 19, 2009: www.alternet.org/sex/143374/rethinking_marriage._the_world_has_changed._it's_time!

13. Associated Press. "Gov't Drops Defense of Anti-Gay Marriage Law." February 23, 2011: http://nhjournal.com/2011/02/23/gov%E2%80%99t-drops-defense-of-anti-gay-marriage-law.

14. Warner, Michael. *The Trouble with Normal: Sex, Politics, and the Ethics of Queer Life* (New York, NY: Free Press, 1999), 82.

{ CHAPTER THREE }

Cinderella 2.0: New Era, Same Old Fairytales

1. Pozner, Jennifer L. *Reality Bites Back: The Troubling Truth about Guilty Pleasure TV* (Berkeley, CA: Seal Press, 2010), 46.

2. Valenti, Jessica. *The Purity Myth* (Berkeley, CA: Seal Press, 2009), 8.

3. Ingraham, Chrys. *White Weddings: Romancing Heterosexuality in Popular Culture* (New York, NY: Routledge, 1999), 38.

4. Winter, Caroline. "What Do Prisoners Make for Victoria's Secret?" *Mother Jones*, July 2008: http://motherjones.com/politics/2008/07/what-do-prisoners-make-victorias-secret.

5. www.change.org/petitions/ask-1-800-flowers-to-offer-fair-trade-flowers-that-arent-picked-by-exploited-workers#?opt_new=t&opt_fb=t.

6. Walt, Vivienne. "Diamonds Aren't Forever." CNN. December 7, 2006: http://money.cnn.com/magazines/fortune/fortune_archive/2006/12/11/8395442/index.htm.

7. Graff, E. J. *What Is Marriage For?* (Boston, MA: Beacon Press, 2004), 40.

8. Kipnis, Laura. *Against Love: A Polemic* (New York, NY: Random House, 2003).

9. Kingston, Anne. *The Meaning of Wife* (New York, NY: Picador, 2004), 3.

{ CHAPTER FOUR }

Top Five Sexist Myths Pushed in Popular Books on Dating

1. Peterson, Latoya. "Steve Harvey: What Women Need to Know." *Salon*, December 24, 2010: www.salon.com/life/feature/2010/12/24/steve_harvey_straight_talk_interview/index.html.
2. hooks, bell. *All About Love* (New York, NY: HarperCollins, 2000), xxiii.
3. Preidt, Robert. "Study: Casual Sex Doesn't Kill Chance of Long-Term Relationship." *USA Today,* September 4, 2010: www.usatoday.com/yourlife/health/medical/2010-09-04-casual-sex-relationships_N.htm.
4. Kerner, Ian. *Be Honest—You're Not That Into Him Either* (New York, NY: HarperCollins, 2005), 73.
5. Berhendt, Greg and Liz Tuccillo. *He's Just Not That Into You* (New York, NY: Simon Spotlight Entertainment, 2004), 16–17.
6. Izrael, Jimi. *The Denzel Principle: Why Black Women Can't Find Good Black Men* (New York, NY: St. Martin's Press, 2010).
7. Stork, Travis L. *Don't Be That Girl* (New York, NY: Simon Spotlight Entertainment, 2008), 144.
8. Argov, Sherry. *Why Men Marry Bitches: A Woman's Guide to Winning Her Man's Heart* (New York, NY: Simon & Schuster, 2006), 2.
9. RAINN. "Who Are the Victims? Breakdown by Gender and Age." www.rainn.org/get-information/statistics/sexual-assault-victims.

{ CHAPTER FIVE }

Single and Lovin' It! Sorta.

1. Rabinovitz, Lauren. "Ms.-Representation: The Politics of Feminist Sitcoms." Television, History, and American Culture: Feminist Critical Essays, (Durham, NC: Duke University Press, 1999), 144–147.
2. "Financial Experience and Behaviors Among Women: 2010–2011." Prudential Research Study.
3. Dougherty, Conor. "Young Women's Pay Exceeds Male Peers," *Wall Street Journal,* September 1, 2010: http://online.wsj.com/article/SB10001424052748704421104575463790770831192.html.
4. McMillan, Tracy. "Why You're Not Married." *Huffington Post,* February 13, 2011: www.huffingtonpost.com/tracy-mcmillian/why-youre-not-married_b_822088.html.

5. Lexington. "Sex and the Single Black Woman." *The Economist:* www.economist.com/node/15867956.

6. Gottlieb, Lori. *Marry Him: The Case for Settling for Mr. Good Enough* (New York, NY: Penguin Books, 2010).

{ CHAPTER SIX }

Nice Guys, Pickup Artists, and the Masculinity "Crisis"

1. Brooks, David. "Mind Over Muscle." *The New York Times*, October 16, 2005: http://query.nytimes.com/gst/fullpage.html?res=9B0DE5D9143FF935A25753C1A9639C8B63.

2. Ode, Kim. "Women Better Educated, But Earn Less Than Men." *Star Tribune*, March 3, 2011: http://new.bangordailynews.com/2011/03/03/business/women-better-educated-but-earn-less-than-men.

3. Rosin, Hanna. "The End of Men." *The Atlantic*, July 2010: www.theatlantic.com/magazine/archive/2010/07/the-end-of-men/8135.

4. Friedman, Ann. "It's Not the End of Men." *The American Prospect*, June 10, 2010: www.prospect.org/cs/articles?article=its_not_the_end_of_men.

5. Clark-Flory, Tracy. "Why Feminism Was Good for Marriage." *Salon*, January 12, 2011: www.salon.com/life/feature/2011/01/12/coontz_qa.

6. Bennhold, Katrin. "Keeping Romance Alive in the Age of Female Empowerment." *The New York Times*, December 1, 2010: www.nytimes.com/2010/12/01/world/europe/01iht-letter.html.

7. Hess, Amanda. "A Brief History of the *New York Times'* Gender Essentialist Trend Piece." *TBD*, December 2, 2010: www.tbd.com/blogs/amanda-hess/2010/12/new-york-times-trends-women-5379.html.

8. Hymowitz, Kay. "Where Have the Good Men Gone?" *Wall Street Journal*, February 19, 2011: http://online.wsj.com/article/SB10001424052748704409004576146321725889448.html.

9. Filipovic, Jill. "Where Have All the Good Men Gone?" *Feministe*, February 21, 2011: www.feministe.us/blog/archives/2011/02/21/where-have-all-the-good-men-gone/.

10. Strauss, Neil. *The Game: Penetrating the Secret Society of Pickup Artists* (New York: HarperCollins Publisher, Inc., 2005).

11. Anonymous. "What to Do if a Girl Says, 'Is That a Line?' *Pick Up Artist Mindset*, December 7, 2010: www.pickupartistmindset.com/bars-clubs/what-to-do-if-a-girl-says-is-that-a-line.

12. Reider, Dimi. "Guys, I Just Totally Raped This Student Chick!" *972*, December 21, 2010: http://972mag.com/guys-i-just-totally-raped-this-student-chick.

13. Thorn, Clarisse. "Well-Known Pickup Artist Allegedly Shoots Woman in the Face." *Feministe*, January 19, 2011: www.feministe.us/blog/archives/2011/01/19/well-known-pickup-artist-allegedly-shoots-woman-in-the-face.

14. Marcotte, Amanda. "These Crimes Don't Happen in a Vacuum." *Pandagon.net*, August 5, 2009: http://pandagon.net/index.php/site/these_crimes_dont_happen_in_a_vacuum.

{ CHAPTER SEVEN }

Dating While Feminist (DWF)

1. Film by Astra Taylor: *Examined Life*, February 2009.

2. Easton, Dossie and Catherine A. Liszt. *The Ethical Slut* (San Francisco, CA: Greenery Press, 1997).

{ CHAPTER EIGHT }

Naughty Girls Need Love Too

1. Editors. *Legal Momentum:* www.legalmomentum.org/our-work/sfr/concerned-women-for-america.html.

2. Valenti, Jessica. *The Purity Myth* (Berkeley, CA: Seal Press, 2009), 23.

3. Sessions Stepp, Laura. *Unhooked: How Young Women Pursue Sex, Delay Love, and Lose at Both* (New York, NY: Penguin Group, 2007).

4. Simmons, Rachel. "Is Hooking Up Good For Girls?" *Rachel Simmons*, February 25, 2010: www.rachelsimmons.com/2010/02/why-the-hook-up-culture-is-hurting-girls.

5. Corinna, Heather. *Scarleteen*, August 4, 2010: www.scarleteen.com/blog/heather_corinna/2010/08/04/pump_up_the_voleume_talking_oxytocin.

6. Clark, Russell D. and Elaine Hatfield. "Gender Differences in Receptivity to Sexual Offers." *Journal of Psychology and Human Sexuality*, 1989.

7. Conley, Terri D. "Perceived Proposer Personality Characteristics and Gender Differences in Acceptance of Casual Sex Offers." *Journal of Personality and Social Psychology*, March 2011.

8. MacAulay Millar, Thomas. "Gender Differences and Casual Sex: The New Research." *Yes Means Yes blog,* March 3, 2011: http://yesmeans yesblog.wordpress.com/2011/03/03/gender-differences-and-casual-sex-the-new-research.

9. Levy, Ariel. *Female Chauvinist Pigs* (New York, NY: Free Press, 2005).

10. Friedman, Jaclyn. *Feministe,* July 26, 2010: www.feministe.us/blog/archives/2010/07/26/my-sluthood-myself.

11. Marcotte, Amanda. "It's Not the Sex, It's the Sexism" *Pandagon,* February 28, 2010. http://pandagon.net/index.php/site/comments/its_not_the_sex_its_the_sexism.

{ CHAPTER NINE }

The Art of Feminist Romantic Maintenance

1. Valenti, Jessica. *Full Frontal Feminism: A Young Woman's Guide to Why Feminism Matters* (Berkeley: CA: Seal Press, 2007).

2. Martin, Courtney E. "Why Love Is Our Most Powerful, Lasting Form of Activism." *AlterNet.org,* February 14, 2007: www.alternet.org/sex/47779.

acknowledgments

Thank you . . .

To Brooke Warner at Seal Press for helping me develop this idea, making this project possible, and putting so much work into ensuring its completion. I know I was not the easiest person to edit, but thank you for believing in me.

To my OG *Feministing* crew:

To Jessica Valenti for pushing me to write when I couldn't even write complete sentences and for opening me up to opportunities that have completely changed my life. I am forever grateful.

To my dear Vanessa Valenti for being such an awesome friend and colleague. I could not have done this without your constant encouragement, site coverage (hello!), and daily chat love.

To Ann Friedman for pushing me to be a better writer, for reminding me that we are fine (and fabulous) just the way we are, even when it gets scary. Single is a lot less scary when your fiercest bitches are too.

To Courtney Martin for sending me an invaluable list of things to remember while writing and constantly telling me to follow my voice. And for telling me in the twenty-fifth hour that you loved what you read—holy crap, that helped.

To Perez for reminding me that I am too hard on myself, and for your ongoing friendship, professional support, and cowork dates. Your calm dedication is an inspiration to me.

To the *Feministing* community, you were the first community that believed in my work. You supported and encouraged me as we all worked together to create the fiercest space of online feminism ever. Thank you.

To my hoomie, Puck, you are the best; you saw the ugliest side of this book project. Thank you for all the late-night convos, for talking me off so many ledges, for saying the unpopular thing even when I didn't want to hear it, and for constantly reminding me that I am going to be okay. I couldn't have done it without you.

To Katie Halper for your last-minute help, employing the much-needed Halperian method to the structure of my chapters, being my taskmaster, fighting with me to make the book awesome, and whipping my ideas into shape. You are damn good. Now let's take over the world.

To Neela for your endless support with this project, reading early drafts and helping me flesh out ideas, and for being the sister of my heart. This book is for those two confused twenty-three-year-olds that met under a table . . . oh so long ago.

To Rebekah for giving me the first bad dating book that inspired me to write this book and for always disagreeing with me. I guess we have yet to see who is right and who is wrong, but at least we'll still be besties.

To my Wifey for having the courage to love radically and for modeling compassion. We struggled through these issues together and our mutual vulnerability and openness to new ways of loving is what makes us wifies.

To Dave for being my best male friend in the world, for reading my stuff even if it is not in your area of interest or expertise, and for sending me so many great tunes to write to.

To Kelly for the encouragement and for showing me that love really can overcome anything.

To Kara for being righteously angry with me when we need to be and for making strategic use of our anger to change the world.

To Kari for growing with me and for showing me what healthy love can look like. And to Olivia, for bigging me up so much and loving one of my best friends so well.

To Erica for never being judgmental, yet so full of insight when it comes to love and life.

To Jessica for being such a good friend, partner in crime, and nerdy girl soul mate.

To Janna for reminding me to be hopeful about love, when I am too analytical and too much in disbelief.

To Lori for the daily chats, for making me write about sex, and for taking so many risks when it comes to love it scares me; it's good for me.

To Twanna for being such an inspiration to me, and a reminder that sexy, single, and loving it is a choice and an act of courage.

To Legba: well, you already know why, but thank you for that and for being you.

To Lisa Fox for constantly yelling at me to finish the damn book.

To Elyse for being so supportive of who I am, not just this year, but for the last thirty.

To Chris Fife: you are a damn good friend—thank you for the pep talks.

To Alex for the support, but please stop writing inappropriate things on my FB.

To Jason: what *is* a girl without her gay? You are such a radiant, positive person—thank you for all the support.

To Sean for sharing with me that you too feel like a hack sometimes. When I talk about being an outsider in high school, I'm thinking about us.

To Rose for always thinking I'm smarter than I am.

To Aminatou for sending me the most encouraging email I have ever received in my life. Luh u boo.

To Chloe Angyal for taking such a tremendous role at *Feministing* while I was in deadline hell, and for reading through chapters.

To Jos Truitt, for being a genius and telling me I am the person you want writing this book.

To Amanda Marcotte for reminding me what people want to hear from me.

To Jay Smooth, my favorite feminist of the male variety—thank you for telling me I "got this."

To Anjali and Rahul Kar, best brother-sister duo ever, thanks for your endless support in what I do.

To Sujata Mitra, thanks for listening to me when I was freaking out on chat and for being so matter of fact, yet so encouraging.

To Neshma Friend for having the courage to be creative.

To Marielle for the last-minute vote of confidence.

To Jaclyn Friedman—holy shit, we did it.

To Latoya Peterson for your endless support and wisdom. Now we can get to work on that sitcom that is going to change the world.

To Jenn Pozner for telling me I couldn't let anyone down and for truly understanding where I was coming from.

To Kristina Rizga for believing in the power of my voice before anyone had really even heard it.

To Jillian Sandell for supporting me as a graduate student and helping me finish my MA thesis so I could get to working on this book. And to

Kasturi Ray, for guiding the completion of my MA thesis. So much of this book is based on the work I did at SF State.

To Russell for telling me to write like an orphan.

To Deanna Zandt, Sonal Bains, Jamia Wilson, Rebekah Spicuglia, Jill Filipovic, Hugo Schwyzer, Thomas Friedman, and Nona Willis Aronowitz: Thanks for all your savvy brilliant quotes, words of encouragement, and support.

To Shakthi Jothianandan for saying "existential feminist dating conundrum." Yeah, that pretty much summed it up.

To my CMJ family: Malkia Cyril, you are my mentor, thank you for your endless wisdom. Karlos Gauna Schmieder, you are one of the smartest, most beautiful people I know—keep writing those poems. Jen Soriano, for showing me what compassionate commitment means. Oshen Turman, your courage, insight, and support mean everything to me. Lisa Jervis, for just understanding where I was coming from and reminding me of the limits of feminism. Mervyn Marcano, you are just impressive and brilliant—thank you for the love. You all are my soul; you keep me real and grounded. Thank you for teaching me the importance of storytelling and reminding me to always follow my voice. And for giving me a place in the movement.

To my SXSW fam: Jason Toney, Lynne d Johnson, Tiffany B. Brown, Cecily Walker, and George Kelly. You guys were all mentors to me about how to tell my story and still monetize.

To Peter Uncle and Diane Auntie for the constant encouragement, not just with this book, but throughout my whole life. I carry your confidence in me with everything I do.

To Bobby, I am so proud of the man you have become. And thanks, Baba, I wouldn't be so into writing if you weren't reading and talking to me about politics my whole life.

To all the amazing students, faculty, and leaders I meet across the country doing the hard daily work of feminist activism and thought pro duction. You make this work possible for me and I am eternally grateful for the opportunity.

To San Francisco, where it all started, and to Brooklyn, where it all came to completion.

To all the people I've ever been romantic with. Yeah, YOU.

ABOUT THE AUTHOR

© DANNY AVILA

SAMHITA MUKHOPADHYAY is a writer, teacher, and speaker residing in Brooklyn, New York. She is the Executive Editor of *Feministing.com,* a popular blog for enthusiasts of feminism. She's not a player, she just crushes a lot.

Selected Titles from Seal Press

For more than thirty years, Seal Press has published
groundbreaking books. By women. For women.

What You Really Really Want: The Smart Girl's Shame-Free Guide to Sex and Safety, by Jaclyn Friedman. $17.00, 978-1-58005-344-0. An educational and interactive guide that gives young women the tools they need to decipher the modern world's confusing, hypersexualized landscape and define their own sexual identity.

The Choice Effect: Love and Commitment in an Age of Too Many Options, by Amalia McGibbon, Lara Vogel, and Claire A. Williams. $16.95, 978-1-58005-293-1. Three young, successful, and ambitious women provide insight into the quarterlife angst that surrounds dating and relationships and examine why more options equals less commitment for today's twentysomethings.

Inappropriate Random: Stories on Sex and Love, edited by Amy Prior. $13.95, 978-1-58005-099-9. This collection of short fiction by women writers takes a hard look at love today—exposing its flaws with unflinching, often hilarious, candor.

No Excuses: 9 Ways Women Can Change How We Think about Power, by Gloria Feldt. $24.95, 978-1-58005-328-0. From the boardroom to the bedroom, public office to personal relationships, feminist icon Gloria Feldt offers women the tools they need to walk through the doors of opportunity and achieve parity with men.

Kissing Outside the Lines: A True Story of Love and Race and Happily Ever After, by Diane Farr. $24.95, 978-1-58005-390-7. Actress and columnist Diane Farr's unapologetic, and often hilarious, look at the complexities of interracial/ethnic/religious/what-have-you love.

The New Latina's Bible: The Modern Latina's Guide to Love, Spirituality, Family, and La Vida, by Sandra Guzman. $19.95, 978-1-58005-358-7. A comprehensive guide that tackles the real-world issues faced by U.S.-born-and-raised Latinas today, from family to dating to the workplace.

Find Seal Press Online

www.SealPress.com

www.Facebook.com/SealPress

Twitter: @SealPress